Breaking Barriers

experiences of a literacy worker in India -
where the unexpected is the norm

Layla Anastasiou

WESTBOW
PRESS®
A DIVISION OF THOMAS NELSON
& ZONDERVAN

WestBow Press books may be ordered through booksellers or by contacting:

WestBow Press
A Division of Thomas Nelson & Zondervan
1663 Liberty Drive
Bloomington, IN 47403
www.westbowpress.com
1 (866) 928-1240

ISBN: 978-1-5127-4215-2 (sc)
ISBN: 978-1-5127-4217-6 (hc)
ISBN: 978-1-5127-4216-9 (e)

Library of Congress Control Number: 2016907817

Print information available on the last page.

WestBow Press rev. date: 05/20/2016

Contents

"For he himself is our peace, who has made the two one and has destroyed the barrier, the dividing wall of hostility ..."

Eph 2:14 NIV

Winging in from beyond my searching eye,
A growing speck, a pulsating white fleck
Against the vastness of the open sky.
Measured heartbeat of easy motion
Serenity so sure, calm without flaw
Passing high above the restless ocean.
Flying on through unlimited spaces.
Where barriers are gone, horizons passed,
Where clouds are dreams and planets have faces.
No longer tied to this earthbound life
Peace alone, time on my own
Free from the bondage of earthly strife.
Up here where silence is serene
There's time to think, time to drink
The essence of peace, reigning supreme.
Flying on, with destination determined,
Sunrise seeking, assurance speaking
With knowledge of what is to come.
No limit to vision, no mountains to ascend.
All is in sight, all in the light
The future stretching beyond the sea's end.

by the author, written about 1979

Foreword

Breaking Barriers reveals the heart of a woman with a passion for lifting non-readers out of the darkness of illiteracy. Layla Anastasiou is a missionary motivated by the love of Christ to teach men and women across India to read so that they can read God's love letter (the Bible) for themselves. She shares her story with complete transparency, showing us the emotions she feels while encountering a myriad of cross-cultural frustrations. Her story is woven through a several-year journey while crafting primers (basic-readers) in different languages and facilitating teacher-training workshops that empower and equip local literacy workers.

Layla has an obedient servant heart, and shares how she has responded to God's call to some of the most impoverished areas on the planet. She shares the plight of non-readers found in extreme poverty and oppression. Her stories include lives transformed through the ability to read God's word, not the least of which includes rescuing trafficked sex workers released from their bondage of illiteracy. Her stories show God's transforming power for individuals' lives as well as for entire villages. Her labor culminates in celebrating new readers reading their very own Bibles.

The complexion of this earth and heaven itself will be forever changed because of the work of Layla and thousands like her. I trust God uses this book to motivate others to do the same. May God continue to give them his strength and grace for the journey ahead.

- Dr. Sidney Venable Rice - President & CEO of Literacy International

Introduction

I have a burden to see people reading the Word of God for themselves so that they may come to know Jesus. I know the power of the Bible because, after I was given a New Testament by the Gideons at the age of 11, the living Lord Jesus saved and changed me when I committed my life to Him at 13.

I went to India when I was in my early 20's and it was after visiting William Carey's college and rooms of the printing press in Serampore in West Bengal and learning about his life and that of his family and colleagues, that I was convinced people actually needed to read God's Word and not rely on second, or third-hand hearsay. In the early nineteenth century he had translated the Scriptures into many Indian languages.

I learnt how to construct primers and how to train teachers when I completed a course in literacy in the U.S.A. in 2005. It did help that I had learnt five languages and that doesn't include my now rusty knowledge of the French that I studied at school. I also have a postgraduate diploma in teaching English as a second language.

My Swiss husband, John*, and I have four wonderful children; two boys and two girls, three of whom were born in Nepal where we lived for eight years. Switzerland became home for us as a family for 16 years and continues to be so for most of our children. Three are now married and our eldest son, his wife and two children are presently living and serving the Lord in Zambia, Africa. Presently we have three grandchildren.

John and I moved to India in 2008. We gained our vision for India through Operation Mobilisation (OM), a group we worked with between 1979 and 1982.

For people who haven't spent time in the Indian subcontinent, you may wonder why there is such a big issue with literacy. Why are people in the twenty-first century still unable to read or write? To answer this would be a book in itself. Schools can be found all over India. Poor children are able to go to the free but very low quality government schools. However, they learn very little and many a time when I visit them, the children are running around in their ragged uniforms with no teacher present. A government job is well-paid whether you go to work or not.

Most of the learners in our literacy classes are young men and women between 20 and 35 years of age. Their most common answer as to why they didn't go to school is either: no time; no opportunity; or there wasn't one. The usual reasons are: because they had to stay at home and work in the house; or work on the land; or work as a child labourer in order for the family to make ends meet. Children are engaged in family businesses in cities and drop out of school after a few short years.

There is no national language in India but 22 languages are officially recognised and there are 30 with over one million speakers. The SIL Ethnologue lists 438 living languages but the 2001 Census of India recorded 122 major languages and 1599 other languages. Sources vary, primarily because of the differences in definition of the terms "language" and "dialect".

During my first five years in India the teams and I constructed primers in the Oriya, Kui, Bengali, Sadri, Gujjari, Apatani, Bhojpuri and Tamil languages.

Oriya (or Odiya) is the state language of Orissa (Odisha) and Kui is both a tribal people group as well as a language in the district of Kandhmal of the same state, which is in the eastern part of India. Bengali is the state language of West Bengal and Sadri is the name of a *scheduled caste* as well as the name of the language, which is spread across West Bengal and spills over into several neighbouring states. The Gujjar people are scattered over North Western India; there are both Muslim and Hindu Gujjar. Apatani is a language spoken by the tribal people of the same name in Arunachal Pradesh in a remote area of North Eastern India. The language or dialect of the Bhojpuri people is widely spread in North India especially in Bihar and Uttar Pradesh. Tamil is the state language of Tamil Nadu and of the Dravidian languages confined to South India. This language family has defied all attempts to show a connection with other languages or language families. The construction of the Tamil primer was an unforgettable headache due to listening to this rumbling language. Having said that, the sophisticated and gracious team was a real joy to work with.

The method we use to construct primers is an eclectic one drawn from celebrated linguists such as Gudschinsky, Laubach and others. Alongside the writing of these education materials, I train local people in Teacher Training Workshops to teach their non-reading neighbours to read and write using the primers we have created. Many people I encounter confuse what I am doing with translation work. The primers are written directly in the given language and are not translations of English or any other language.

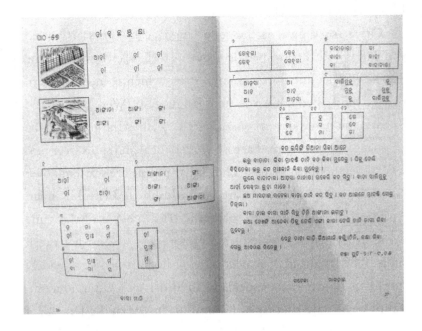

The syntax of most north Indian languages is very similar. As I had learnt Hindi it was easier to "take on" another language and its orthography, and to familiarise myself with the consonant and vowel patterns, diacritics etc. Their scripts are all syllabaries. However, we used the Roman alphabet for the Apatani. A syllabary makes for a more exact rendering of the sound to written symbol, e.g. how should you pronounce "ho"?— ho like the English word hoe / həʊ/ or ho like the first part of the word hot /hɒ/? Whereas in a syllabary it would be phonetically clear होउ or हो (Devanagri) and ଜୋଉ or ଜୋ Oriya (Kalinga script).

Each primer is made up of two volumes; the first is created by local people using limited vocabulary and is, therefore, limited to simple stories. The second volume includes an initial 10 or 12 health, agriculture and self-help lessons followed by 36 simplified Bible stories.

There has been a concentrated effort during the last two years to see the quantity and quality of classes increase in Kandhmal, and to train a couple of individuals to hold Teacher Training Workshops themselves. I find myself always having to be right behind them, checking again and again.

When I am at home in North India I teach English at the Bible College where John is a Bible teacher. I spend a lot of time travelling to distant parts of India to do literacy work.

The following narrative describes events as they unfold in the lives of literacy teachers, as well as those who have accompanied me along the way during the writing of adult literacy primers.

To protect some of those I have worked with I have changed their names and the names of the places where they live. *My husband's and my own name have also been changed.

The chapters were originally written as letters to interested friends around the world. This is why they read as if the events were happening in present time.

1

Arrival in the Lofty Heights of the Himalayas—written in February 2008

We arrived in India at the beginning of February 2008. Our first seven weeks were spent in a freezing cold house belonging to friends who were enjoying a better climate somewhere else. This house was 2,500 metres above sea level in the foothills of the Himalayas close to Mussoorie.

This was originally a hill station on the ridge of several hills, founded and established by the British Raj in the nineteenth century for military personnel and their families. We found a congested town that in summer attracted hundreds of Indian tourists trying to escape the heat of Delhi. When the British first arrived, no one lived in the area since there was no water. The first thing they did was to search for and find water far down below and create a system to get it up. Much of the infrastructure from all those years ago still remains. The plumbing in these old cottages has outlasted many of the modern Indian "experiments" that you have to live with elsewhere.

We spent almost two months learning Hindi all day and every day, and that has been of great benefit.

After that, we searched and finally found a house to rent in a different part of the state of Uttarakhand. We were very happy with it, but it wasn't very easy. House owners raised the rent as soon as we showed interest, and even after moving in, the landlord tried to change it. But all is settled, and we have kept a good relationship with him. Two days after moving in, primer construction began.

Creating a Reader for the Gujjar People—written in May 2008

The Gujjar are a semi nomadic people spread over a very large area of northern India that includes the states of Jammu and Kashmir, Rajasthan, and the area around Delhi, Uttar Pradesh, and our home state of Uttarakhand.

Three Americans, a former Hindu Brahmin Indian who works among the Gujjar people, three Gujjars, and I got down to 15 days of solid work in May creating the adult readers. We worked from 8am till 6:30pm, with one-hour breaks for lunch. It was difficult for the Gujjar jungle people to sit at a table for such a long time, and only two of them could read.

This project was a great endeavour as the Gujjar had not had their language written down until then. So we had no other materials to work with. They pronounced the words and we wrote them down using the Devanagari script, not the Arabic script. This was their express wish, even though they are Muslims.

As we progressed into the last volume of the primer, which included simplified Bible stories, the Gujjar Muslim co-workers became very uneasy. They were always aware of what was involved, and it was they who had requested that these materials be created. They had, however, been home since the work started, so religious leaders and others from outside the tribe had got to know about the project, and our Gujjar friends had become fearful. They demanded that on no account must the name of Jesus Christ be mentioned! But at least a quarter of the primer included New Testament stories.

We were grateful that Brother Faizal arrived at that time. He is a key man who has a passion to bring the good news to the Gujjar people. He turned up one day out of the blue, and we were able to link him up with the work of literacy.

Faizal grew up in a Koranic school in North India, and he had known nothing other than the Koran. He is fluent in Arabic, Urdu, Hindi, and Nepali, and is quite good in English too. Before becoming a Christian he was a mullah and was actively spreading Islam in Nepal. Standing in our living room clad in *salwar kurta* and with his long beard, he demonstrated to us the call to prayer. He sang this in a rather woeful Arabic tune, which to him was very beautiful.

He told us that after one of his missionary campaigns he was returning to Kathmandu from Delhi. The bus stopped for breakfast in one of the mountain towns in Nepal. While eating, three Nepali Christians started talking to him about the Lord Jesus. He became very angry with them and was so zealously preaching his Muslim faith that the bus left without him, taking his entire luggage, which included many kilos of Islamic books.

He was then, needless to say, furious with those Christians. He was eager to catch the next bus in the hope of catching up with the original one to get his luggage back. In the evening he was at a Muslim restaurant beside a mosque. While eating, the television news came on announcing the tragic story of a bus that had gone over the side of a mountain—and everyone in it had died. They actually read out all the names from the register office list of those who had been aboard the bus, and his own name was among the dead. He was in terrific shock as he realised what had happened. In his shocked state of mind, he blurted out to the man sat opposite him that he should have been in that bus. The man opposite said, "Well, praise the Lord!" And so another believer was put in his path! This man was able to share the good news with him, and Faizal understood that it was the Lord who had saved him and that the Lord was Jesus. The man led him to faith, and afterward Faizal was nurtured for several years by a leading Nepalese pastor.

Being a Muslim mullah (or so his family still thought), Faizal was called back to India by his father to preach at his sister's wedding. When they found out what had happened, his father beat him so badly that he almost died. His clothes were in shreds, and he had to leave the house bleeding, without shoes, and just about naked. He showed us the scars on his face.

Sometime later he went to Bible school in South India. While in the south, he was able to lead a number of Muslims to the Lord, including two other mullahs and an imam. The imam has since become a Christian pastor. Faizal suffered such a lot of opposition there. Muslims tried to throw acid at his face, but fortunately he was able to dodge out of the way. Twice he was stabbed in the chest, and once he was poisoned. God saved him each time. He was warned to flee for his life because his death was imminent. So one night he fled with his wife and two sons. They arrived in our town one month later.

After I heard his testimony, I dared myself to share with him the difficulty we were having with the local religious leaders and their control over the Gujjar. It was then that he told me that he believed he had been called by Jesus to work with the Gujjar people.

How I praise God for all of these events! And how thrilling it is to be part of His plan. Faizal told us a lot more concerning the Koran and the transformative power of the Bible. It's my hope that he will be used amongst the leaders of the Gujjar.

We decided it might be best to put all the New Testament stories in a separate volume that could be used with those who wanted to continue reading after completing the first two books.

2

On a Sri Lankan Beach—
written in August 2008

I've noticed a certain cynicism creeping over me over the months—where I inwardly mock God's servants for attributing positive turns of events to God's working. I explained away people's testimonies in church as nature merely taking its course. I realised, horrified, that this was pure unbelief in the Almighty.

"What can I do?" I asked God.

When prayers were not answered, I inwardly thought, *See! There's proof again that prayer is all in vain.*

When prayers were answered, I rationalised the reason in a humanistic way. I suppose it's typical of many westerners.

When our children were growing up in Nepal, I felt like the persistent widow in the Bible nagging the judge for justice (Luke 18). I nagged God with my petitions through all the children's sicknesses to be sure He would answer—and He did!

Recently I have felt more like Jonah. God has done amazing miracles over the years, leaving me in no doubt about what He can and does do. Yet, like Jonah, I moaned about something small like the vine that grew up, provided shade, and promptly died—leaving Jonah cynical and contemptuous. Nineveh had repented when Jonah would rather that they had all been thrown into hell.

What to do?

My husband, John, and I had left India due to the expiration of our tourist visas. We were trying out the Indian Embassy in Sri Lanka, hoping for a student visa since these are usually given for longer periods. This would mean we wouldn't have to keep leaving the country. A school in India had provided us with a letter of recommendation, saying we were enrolled for one year. I asked the school to change it to two.

At the embassy in Sri Lanka, the attaché asked, "How long do you want—two years?"

We said, "Oh, at least two."

I added, "At least three!"

"What, two years and three months?" he asked.

"No," I said, "three years." So he wrote three years but said we would have to get clearance from Switzerland.

While waiting for clearance we visited several places, including Paradise Beach. This is a beautiful, palm-fringed beach, but during the monsoon season the sea is extremely wild. The waves crash night and day, and there is no let-up whatsoever.

We sat on the sand and prayed for various people and problems. One problem was that the people who were renting our house in Switzerland hadn't paid the rent for at least five months. As we prayed, the same cynical attitude crept over me. Inwardly I prayed for help and for forgiveness. I prayed above all for God to increase my faith.

The next day we decided to walk the length of the beach. John had been lying on a mat so he left his glasses and book on it. I put my sunglasses down on it as well because I didn't want to lose them in the rough sea. My sunglasses were precious to me because they were made to suit my eyes—not ordinary sunglasses.

When we returned we noticed our stupidity. The wind had blown the mat down the beach and everything with it. I found John's glasses within a few minutes sticking up out of the wet sand as the water receded. "Praise God," he shouted, and started worrying about his book.

What about my glasses? Immediately I remembered that I had prayed for an increase in faith. I scoured the area, digging up the sand, and searching the bushes. Finally the thin strip of beach was covered by the incoming tide. The rest of the day the waves pounded that thin shore line. Rain and storms came and went. At the end of the day I was mad with God because I had believed I would find them but hadn't. I had prayed for increased faith;, I had sought, but not found.

When we were praying in the evening, John said, "What, do you expect them to come right out of that ocean into your hands?"

"I don't care how, but I had believed and thought this was how God was testing my faith."

Late that night we phoned our friend who was dealing with our house rent issue. He sounded very relaxed, and said that three months had now been paid and the tenants had assured him the rest was on the way. So why was I still bothered about so small a thing as a pair of sunglasses? I was adamant. Why hadn't God answered my expectant faith?

"Perhaps He will," John said and slept.

Next morning we were walking from the little hut to breakfast. My mind was hazy as I hadn't slept much. I only took one glance at the sea and shore. Something was sitting delicately on the wet beach ... I literally couldn't believe my eyes ... You've guessed it ... my sunglasses—nicely folded, wet but not scratched and looking positively perfect! I was incredulous. We were both stupefied, and so were all the staff who had searched with us!

Why, after all these years did I need a miracle to happen? I don't know. Maybe it revealed my slow spiritual growth. It showed me again that everything was in God's hands. Many terrible things happen that we cannot understand, yet all this is in His hands.

After several more visits to the embassy and a lot of waiting we finally got our three-year student visas.

3

A Very Happy Day of my Life in 1980 (In memory of Graham Staines)

The following recalls a very vivid and precious day in my memory of a very special person.

We left the OM base in Balasore, Orissa (Odisha) waving goodbye to John Brown the Field Leader. Bernice, who was Canadian, Shirley Khan, a Malaysian, and I were on our way to Bangladesh.

It was another wonderful day in India. Hot and sunny, people buying and selling, shop fronts open, bicycle bells ringing, cows chewing, children playing and my white Ford Transit van going. My team vehicle, an ex-hot dog van from England, had to leave India for six months. For those not with OM in India in the 1970s and 1980s this might sound strange, but the law was that any foreign-registered vehicle could not stay in the country continuously for more than six months in a year. Whoever's name the car was registered under was the person who had to drive it out of the country. And so we were off to Dhaka—only

653 kilometres. Not far really. Why we stopped for *chai* (tea) so soon after leaving the base I can't remember; perhaps we hadn't had breakfast but we had hardly driven one hour. I do remember joyfully leaving the *chai* shop (known as a hotel) and climbing back into the driver's seat.

The diesel motor's reassuring clatter sounded promising … First gear, second gear, third … and the gear stick disappeared. Just like that. Maybe there was still something of the teenager in us because we found it very funny and just sat there laughing. Never mind the fact that we had no idea how to fix it, although I did know how to change a wheel and a fan belt. I got out of the van and stuck my head underneath it. The entire gear box was sitting comfortably on the road. I somehow managed to heave it up so that the gear stick reappeared inside the van. Bernice and Shirley were holding on to it for dear life. Back in the driver's seat, looking at this huge lump of metal and then outside at the endless Odisha countryside, I could see that there was no hope of finding any wonderful *Sardarjis* (Sikh men who can fix anything).

But right there in front of me was a signpost: "Baripada 30km" Wasn't that the home of Graham Staines? Graham was a missionary from a bygone era, or that's the way I viewed this Australian bachelor. He had recently spoken to a large group of OMers during a study seminar in Balasore, and I distinctly remembered him saying that he lived in Baripada. So somehow, with one of us steering, one holding the gearbox in place, and one yanking the gears into position, we inched our way to the small town.

The town was very busy and dirty, and we had no idea where Graham lived. But as miracles do happen, one of the first people we spotted was Graham, tall and pale, at least two heads taller than the sea of Indian faces on the street. He was standing outside an oily tool shop. We quickly explained the situation, and he got us and the van to his home on the beautiful Baptist Mission Compound. We were invited in to the lovely cool house where we were served a simple Indian meal and were told to take rest, while he stayed outside in the very hot mid-day sun and fixed my van.

I had heard about his leprosy clinic. Was he a doctor, a mechanic or a gardener or all of these things? He mended the Ford Transit all too soon. Was he a miracle worker or what? He spoke so little and worked so much. We felt embarrassed knowing that this would have been a whole day's work at a huge cost for us had we ended up anywhere else. And, of course, he would not accept any money. He showed us the garden around the house. It was full of all kinds of fruit trees. Mangoes were ripe and he told a young man to cut some for us. Everything I looked at was done beautifully. Every plant and tree was carefully trenched in the rich red soil in preparation for the monsoon rains. The spacious house with its wooden beams was designed so well. The whole place was like a Garden of Eden on the verge of an ugly town.

Amazed, I started up the engine and drove the van around. It was in perfect working order. How do you repay such people? Laughing and praising the Lord, we thanked him and continued on our journey. We decided that he was actually an angel. And this is how I like to remember him.

4

Odisha: No Go!—written in September 2008

When we planned our family trip to Nepal and India in 1999, the place I wanted to take everyone to, most of all, was Odisha. I had kept in contact with Graham Staines over the years, and I greatly respected and admired him. He had written to me encouraging us to visit him at his mission. He had married since we had last met and we could get to know his young family. Just as I was phoning India to make the final plans, I was informed that Graham had been killed—set on fire with his two young sons by Hindu fanatics.

We didn't go to Odisha.

Now, living in India, for the second time I was geared up to go; this time with all my work packed, ready to meet the team and to write the primer for the non-readers—especially the Christians of Odisha. Just in time, a phone call came from our pastor friend in Odisha telling me, in no uncertain terms, not to come. The same fate that had been dealt to Graham, Philip and Timothy Staines was being unleashed on the Christians by those with the same fanatical Hindu beliefs.

I haven't gone to Odisha.

After hearing nothing for a week, my co-worker and I finally got news that our pastor friend and his family had made it to Bhubaneshwar and had escaped into another state.

At the time of writing Odisha is burning. Christians have been raped, killed by burning or murdered in other very brutal ways. Thousands are trying to survive by hiding in the jungle during heavy monsoon rains. When things cool down, we plan to go and give practical help. How I thank God for alerting me just in the nick of time. Had I boarded the plane and landed in Odisha, who knows what may have happened?

5

The Challenges of Constructing a Primer in Oriya—written in February 2009

Five-and-a-half months after the atrocities in Kandhmal, Odisha, I left Delhi by plane on February 14th (having taken the night train from our town to get there). I arrived in Bhubaneshwar, the capital of Odisha, and spent one or two nights there. Bhubaneswar is one of the very few clean cities I have seen in India. Only in this state are the walls bordering the manicured grass verges along the major roads decorated with beautiful, original artwork. Certainly not what I had expected!

Our venue for the primer construction had been changed from the violent Kandhmal district to Gopalpur which is near the ocean. We were able to rent a Catholic-owned centre, purpose-built for workshops and the like. I can't exactly say how many were on our team because it varied daily which was disappointing.

We had exactly two weeks in which to get the work done. This was, by far, not enough time. It was hard going getting the team to understand the concept—to get the big picture. My co-worker, Akash from West Bengal, and I were more than a little exasperated at times. But as the days went by, and the team saw how much we had to get through, they slowly and eventually put their shoulders to the task. We had to create 90 lessons and stories. My work was to know how to break down the words, and then fill in the boxes. This was no small matter in an unknown language in a totally unfamiliar script! Akash could understand a little of the language as it sounded a bit like his own Bengali, though it's script is very different. So he was understanding Oriya (somewhat) and I was reading and writing (somewhat). And so, like this, we were able to control the input of the team as they created the stories, allowing very limited letters and words at first, and then slowly increasing these as the lessons progressed. Due to the team's limitations, ridiculous sentences were often produced and, if we didn't catch them, they would go unnoticed into the book.

Here are two examples: "Grandmother and monkey went from the jungle to the Himalaya by ship!" Or, "Come out of the Himalaya and put a seat out for the politician!"

We worked every day from 9am till after 11.00pm, and I never got much sleep either.

Sadly our typist never materialised so I had two, thick, hand- written files to be corrected and typed before going to the publishers.

As I have already mentioned, the number of team members fluctuated—some arriving at a later date. The following is taken straight from my diary:

Odisha team: during the night

The "ladies" have finally arrived on the team! Two young girls … Within five minutes of their arrival one of them—Sapna—told me her family's life story. Her father died in 1999 and following that three of her siblings have also since died. They were five children but only she and her younger brother are left. They all had an inherited disease from their father—a blood disorder—she said "not enough blood" and then the understatement: "Mother is very sad." Both girls are from Phulbani District, Kandhmal.

The next morning before breakfast, Nitu, the other girl told me how her grandmother was killed by elephants.

Hardly any sleep last night. This is getting to be a rhythm. Went to bed at 11pm. In the middle of the night "music" from across the field started up: a woman's high pitched voice sounded as if she were being forced to sing while standing on a bed of red hot coals. Right after that the water began coming. I couldn't take "bath" last night because there was no more water. Now it was running and the next room toilet's tap had been left on. I rushed out to switch it off and bumped into a man—I think the caretaker who was just coming out. I told him in Hindi that the water's being lost. And he gave me one of those blank puja looks which leave you wondering. I went back to bed and then some man—(I think the caretaker) started singing a bhajan and praying really loudly. I couldn't tell if it was Christian or Hindu, but the people who run this place are Catholic. He went on and on, his bad singing resounding through the night. Just when I thought it was finished everyone started visiting the next door toilet. Coughs and splutters.

Next moment Nitu nudged me to say tea had come and there was a minute cup of sweet black tea on the floor next to my string bed. Right then Sapna decided to get up and wash clothes. That took forever and

17

I was getting desperate because there would soon be no water left again. Lying on the bed I was wondering what to do for the best. For a minute there was peace and then, lo and behold, Beethoven's 5th Symphony came bellowing out of one of the rooms!

The girls took the clothes in the one and only bucket to hang out. When it finally returned, I rushed into the bathroom to grab the moment for a "bath" but the bucket had turned purple—they had been dying clothes! Is this the normal routine during primer construction? I ask you! So I took a purple bath and looking "blue" went to breakfast."

Gopalpur-on-Sea, Odisha
(Don't all book at once!)

During this primer construction we had a half-day off. At about 4pm the men managed to rouse themselves and we all went to Gopalpur-on-Sea, which was just a couple of miles down the road.

A very broken auto rickshaw came to get us, as Akash was very keen that no one would see me coming from the building. We got in and out several times of it within one hundred metres of the house. After all, there were seven of us and then the driver as well, and it was only meant to take three. What a joke. Where there had once been head and back lights, it just had rusty-edged holes like huge eyeless sockets.

The little coloured thatched houses on the way were charming but the people reminded me of the rag-pickers who lived in my part of India. Several men were keen to tell me those people were "Telegu" from Andhra Pradesh.

On arrival, we saw a featureless building with the words "Gopalpur-on-Sea Hotel". After the hotel there was a paved area, about 50 metres long, that was supposedly the promenade. It had a low wall, perhaps with the intention of keeping out the mating and fighting pariah dogs. A typical Indian piece of artwork stood at one end: a concrete fisherman in a concrete boat. He was in a cross-legged position. However, his lower legs had been knocked off and so had his arms. The sculptor had not given him clothes so he looked in a very desperate state. At the other end were very stiff-looking concrete dolphins in a concrete pool. Only instead of water in the pool there was a very thick layer of rubbish. This mini promenade had steps reaching down to the beach. Food vendors were everywhere, and I went to the edge to see the sea. Instead of shore and ocean, it was the crowds which arrested my attention. I wanted to get straight back into the rickshaw, but it had left.

Of course everyone was dressed in their Sunday best, and everyone was eating (and throwing the waste straight down into the sand). Red betel nut spit was everywhere.

As we edged between the crowds of people, trying to get to the shoreline, Akash noticed someone in the sand.

"Is he dead?" He wasn't asking me but just thinking out loud.

"No, I'm sure he's just drunk," I said. A man was lying in an odd position with his face down in the sand. He was facing downhill as the beach sloped steeply to the water's edge. His legs were uphill and his head downhill.

"No I think he's dead," Akash replied.

We walked north along the beach away from the people. Here the rubbish was replaced by the open toilet used by

Gopalpur-on-Sea's fishermen and dogs. As it was yet to be flushed by the monsoon rains, the stench was putrid. It was hard to find a clean space to walk. Then we came across the carcass of a giant turtle.

We turned back.

Yet again, I was struck by the most magnificent sunset, defying the circumstances here on earth below. Sapna and Nitu told me it was one of the best days of their lives.

6

The Infamous Sadri— written in March 2009

When I left Gopalpur-on-Sea I went via Bhubaneswar to Calcutta (Kolkata) in West Bengal for a few days and met up with some old friends. From Kolkata I took a night train to Hashimara where I was met by a pastor and brought to Hamiltonganj. On a map you will see that this part of West Bengal is a narrow strip leading you through into the North-Eastern states of India. It lies between Bhutan to the north and Bangladesh to the south.

John had also just arrived, and was preparing for three weeks of pastors' training and other meetings in the environs. One day he set out prepared for a pastors' meeting, but was met by an expectant group ranging in age from seven years to over 60! A typical situation in rural India. He had more than a few challenges, but I think he enjoyed it very much.

Hamiltonganj is a small place which was established by the British Raj, and is in a tea-growing area. Everyone who visits India should visit this corner of the country. Not only is it very beautiful, but it will make you appreciate your next cup of tea more than ever before. The tea pickers pluck the top new leaves of the bushes by hand and throw them into the basket (*doko*) on their backs, which is held in place by a rope around their foreheads. The people (mostly women) are either Nepali or Sadri. The Sadri of this area is a people-group of about eight to ten million. Till now they have no written language and, although some of the children have the chance to study in Bengali or Hindi medium schools, they are almost all illiterate. Many have come to faith in Jesus, and one Sadri pastor expressed the churches' desire to be able to read the Bible in their own language. The Bible has been translated but not yet printed. After much thought and prayer, we decided to go ahead and write a primer.

John and I stayed in the home of this Sadri pastor and his lively family. The church building is attached to the house. Sunday came and, at a glance, you could read the simplicity of these church peoples' lives. They were mostly tea-pickers or labourers. Almost none could read and all were exuberant when we explained why we had come. (They have, however, created the most wonderful songs of worship to Jesus in their language and, as always in India, they are excellent drummers.) At the end of the service the pastor reminded them to go home in the same *chapals* (flip-flops) and shoes they had come in!

The Sadri people in this part of India told me of their lively and colourful past: their forefathers were murderers of a special kind. They behaved like the highwaymen of Old England. They would join a caravan of unassuming travellers and when the moment was ripe they would strangle their victims to death with their *rumal*— a handkerchief or headscarf. They then robbed their victims and either buried them or threw them in a well. This went on for hundreds of years. They became known as *Thugee* which is a Hindi word for "deceiver" and from which we get the word "thug" in English.

Membership was passed on from father to son or if someone got to know a *thugee* band, he might be recruited if he had the self-discipline required. Sometimes they took the children of the murdered travellers into their group and trained them to become *thugees*. They saw it as an elite profession. They worked in large organised groups and were greatly feared all those years ago. The *thugees* were a tight-lipped band whose secrecy was key to their success for a very long time. But when the British began ruling India, they set up a dedicated police force that was able to hunt down these terrorists. When they caught some of the *thugees*, they allowed them to save their own lives by giving information on their accomplices. This was the beginning of the end of a greatly feared, huge, organised criminal underclass that had murdered thousands and thousands of people.

Now as I walked along with them they laughed about their past showing me that their headscarves were firmly wrapped around their heads in turbans.

We had quite a large team for the Sadri primer which included a couple who came from abroad to work with us. It was much easier to write than the Oriya as we used the Devanagari script just as we would for Hindi. Unfortunately this primer construction took over three weeks to complete due to not having an overview of what was going on with the typist's computer! Too many new words were creeping into the stories too fast. At least by the end of it all, it was nearer to going to the publishers than the Oriya primer.

In all this work, God gave me much grace to endure when I thought the task was becoming truly impossible. I enjoyed a totally Indian diet and experienced excellent health. Everyone went to extremes to make sure I had good water to drink. I was blessed with really good friendships and loved being part of a team.

7

Writing for the Apatani— written in May 2009

At the time of writing I am in a plane flying high above the most amazing Brahmaputra River!

I am returning from Assam having just spent the last two weeks writing for the Apatani tribe of Arunachal Pradesh. For me this has probably been the most successful primer construction to date.

Sadly we weren't allowed to enter Arunachal State itself— because of me being a foreigner. I'm told that the people themselves would welcome outsiders with open arms, but the Indian government doesn't allow it. The same is true for most of the North-Eastern states (at the time of writing). So the team assigned for the job came to Assam.

We had two weeks of very intensive work. The team members were, dare I say it, a totally different calibre of people. They were "tribals" and a different race to those of mainland India. They looked more Chinese than Indian—or somewhere in-between. They were highly motivated and thoroughly dedicated. They seemed to glow with a love for the Lord. We never once had to coax them to work; in fact they stayed up longer in the evenings than either my co-worker or myself. We worked on average from 8am to around 9 or 10pm with a short break over lunch.

The Apatani language belongs to the Sino-Tibetan family. It's a tonal language where the meaning of the same word changes in accordance with the tone. It contrasts vowel and consonant length. Fluent Apatani language speakers are only about 20 per cent of the total population which means this is a very vulnerable language. Nevertheless, it was technically an easy primer to do as we used the Roman script plus a few more symbols—only about 29 letters in all. It went so smoothly that I was able to write in the words and syllables in the template directly into the computer as opposed to writing everything by hand first.

Having said that, I have to add that we worked in the most difficult of circumstances: The heat and humidity was overpowering, and for more than half the time we had no electricity. When the fans went off the sweat flowed like rivulets. If the fans were off in the evening, insects of a thousand varieties would descend on us and especially on the computer screen. Assam has giant orange grasshoppers, large as a man's hand which fly or leap from high into your hair; enormous black beetles and the biggest red cockroaches ... You name it—Assam has it. This place is also famous for being a malaria area; in fact, one of the initial team members had malaria on arrival and had to return home. One night the guys found a large snake in their bedroom. Fortunately it wasn't poisonous. But one evening while we were working (in the church building), Akash, my co-worker, almost stepped on a yellow and green snake which was of a deadly kind. They were able to kill it before it killed him.

One day it was impossibly hot and I wondered whether people would pass out from not being able to breathe properly. My phone stopped working (it was totally wrecked). My UV water filter stopped working, my mouse used up its batteries and my computer gave up—all at the same time! Hallelujah—the computer only stopped for half an hour!

No one could sleep that night, and there was no electricity, and just when I thought I could bare it no longer—it happened. Ear-splitting thunder bolts, lightning, gale force winds—no, it wasn't the end of the world, but the monsoon had been hailed in! It was as if God had drawn back massive vault doors that, until then, had been tightly shut between heaven and earth. The rain came in such torrents that I couldn't even see the trees just across the compound. What an exhilarating experience. I was sure the earth would fall in, but I couldn't contain myself and had to run out into it.

The three humble cooks from the Baptist Mission who looked after us found it very worrying that I couldn't swallow even a third of the rice that the others were so easily consuming. Very sweetly and discreetly they would slide a saucer with a few slices of bread, or two chapattis or a tiny piece of fish next to my plate to supplement my rice.

One evening the guys were busy killing the great grasshoppers by throwing them hard down on the ground. I half consciously noticed them being piled up on the work table. Half an hour later they ended up on our dinner table—deep fried! They couldn't get me to eat one, but I did learn to eat the strangest of fish which looked more like fat worms.

The team made a very deep impression on me. They were sharp minded, and understood very quickly what we were asking of them. But I also noticed that they were incredibly thin and obviously poor. As I got to know more about them it seemed to me that the Apatani tribe were a forgotten people. There are 50,000 of them and they are spread over a district called Ziro! If that sounds like the end of the earth you're not far off. The state is the most easterly in India bordering Tibet and Burma up in the Himalayas. The first time they were introduced to formal education was in 1954 using only the Hindi language. Hindi is as different to them as Chinese is to English. Until now their own language has not been written down save for the gospels of Mark and John and a hymn book using Roman script. So they were over the moon to be part of the creation of a tool that will enable their people to read the up-and-coming Bible in their own language. That we could facilitate this effort was a great privilege for us.

They felt deprived of many things by the Indian government, yet they were not at all bitter. There are also strict anti-conversion laws in Arunachal Pradesh state.

On the last night, at around midnight, one fellow, who was also the Apatani Bible translator, was furiously typing out the last items as we were putting everything together in my computer. No one would go to bed because everyone was trying his hardest to help get finished. They sang songs—anything to keep us going. What great team spirit! It was a very emotional farewell to say the least. Their child-like faith and transparent characters moved me deeply. Now it's my goal to get a permit to see them in their own state and do a Teacher Training Workshop.

8

Diwali in our Town— written in November 2009

Have you ever stood near a thundering waterfall or heard the roar of an avalanche? Continuous, constant falling rocks or crashing water, the roaring going on and on and on. Well that's Diwali! Not rocks or water but fireworks! Never have I experienced fireworks like this—so many, so frequently, for so long, and from dusk to dawn. It's now the third night and, though today is the main day, it's certainly not the final night of banging and lightning. For a time you keep saying "wow!" at the rainbow colours, the variety, the shapes. Then a couple of hours pass and you say, "Well, Indians really do love to celebrate." Then, after another hour, you can't help admire their endurance. But then five, six and more hours pass and it's only getting louder, if that's possible, and you start to wonder about their minds.

If our town is representative of a typical Indian town, then billions and billions of rupees have gone up in smoke these last few days.

We have moved house again and now live on the edge of the town with wonderful views of the hills and forests. I am really enjoying the amazing variety of birds around us. There are too many to list but my favourites have to be the parrots and sun birds. In the mornings we wake up to the very jungly sound of peacocks.

We live amongst some attention-grabbing people too. Our landlady comes through our house rather a lot at the weekends when she is not in Chandigarh. She goes straight to the fridge and helps herself, and this will continue until she has had the stairs built outside. Then she will be able to access her room on the roof and her *Puja* room on the veranda without disturbing us. That's the theory of it.

She has been divorced for two years; she and her husband spent the time building this house and then, when it was ready to move in, they divorced. He tried to kill her by firing his pistol at her (ex-high-up military man) but missed and hit the wall as he was very drunk. Building a house in this country makes or breaks you.

According to Nisha the divorce was due to a variety of inauspicious events in her husband's astrological make up. One event on the list was that he was born on the wrong day of the week. I didn't, of course, dare to suggest that perhaps her neurotic temperament might have helped. She is obsessed with her religion and she should be, for after all she's an educated Brahmin. (Our last landlord was an illiterate nobody.)

As she walked through the other day, I mentioned to her that I'd just been on the phone to our eldest son, and that he couldn't decide when exactly to get married.

"Oh, I can help you," she offered. She knows a very good pundit who can read the signs well, and I just need to give him a few facts about Joel and his fiancée, such as which month and day of the week they were born on, and we should take it from there. (I don't think our son or his fiancée bought the idea).

She stands on the veranda each morning at the weekends and screams a volley of orders to the workmen below, trying to get them moving. It sounds like something major has gone wrong but it always sounds like that.

We also have a young woman who came with the house when we moved in. She cleans the floor on all fours (won't use the mop), and then goes home. I have managed to show her how to wash dishes, but it's all hit-and-miss and she is very limited. She is one of the very desperate ones. She's 23 but looks about 12. She has a drunkard for a husband and three miniscule children. She also has a one-eyed "adopted" girl of about seven years. Each day I expect her to come and tell me one has died.

These two women with two extremely different lives are buzzing in my house and my head constantly. One moment I'm trying to teach one to read, and the next moment the other is asking for advice about how she should best spend her money. Talking to either of them about my faith and what's written in God's Word falls on very deaf ears. Both are utterly devout, and both are terribly lonely and unhappy. So many are like this; yet tonight the celebrations must be wilder than ever before. Nothing makes sense.

9

Crossing India from Pune to Kolkata to Bhimtal— written in August 2010

When anyone mentions the name of the city **Pune,** the idea of a pleasant place comes to mind. It is known as the cultural capital of Maharashtra, the state which has Mumbai as its capital. Mumbai is India's trending chic city and is known for the Bollywood film industry. In contrast, Pune is known for its rich, historical past, twinned together with its modern and vibrant present. In history Pune was part of a large territory ruled by the Mughal Empire. Battles were continuously fought between the Mughals and the Marathas, and Pune changed hands a number of times in the 1600s. It became the political centre of the Maratha Empire in the eighteenth century. Now it attracts people from other parts of India, as well as other parts of Asia and even from Africa and the Middle East. This is due to its research institutes of information technology (IT), automobile manufacturing and many other industries.

The industry that I came across, however, was of a clandestine nature, and not one that Pune would wish to boast about. I had a Teacher Training Workshop, organised by a young Nepalese man called Janga, in order to reach the Nepali Diaspora in India. One trainee took me to her target group: sex workers in downtown Pune. India has really changed; in the past this would all have been furtively carried out. No man would want to have been seen going into these places. Now, neither he, nor anyone else it seemed, could care less. Hundreds of these women were standing outside, casually waiting for clients. Those who were unable to pay the rent, for one reason or another, were locked in tiny cage-like rooms on the roof, and hopefully their clients would go directly there because they would not be able to get out until the rent was paid.

The earnings of all these women go straight to a pimp, and he or she pays the owner of the building who also is heavily involved in the business. The women get a minimal amount of food to eat as wages and maybe some pocket money.

The Nepali women have either been stolen from or sold by their families, whereas the Indian ones are given by their families into prostitution as a sacrifice to their goddess Yellama. The trainee literacy worker who took me there had opened a beauty salon across the road where she shares the Gospel without any inhibitions to those who come to her. So far she has managed to rescue five or seven women (I can't remember exactly how many)

After this I went over to the opposite side of India: to **Kolkata.** I was unable to visit many classes as the teachers were busy preparing for a church programme for Independence Day. Here in India you may plan something with the concerned people, but plans are not taken seriously until you actually arrive. In this case, Independence Day plans came into their minds at a later stage, so therefore our plans were simply ignored. However, one class in downtown New Market, run by two local young women, was in full swing. A rat the size of a cat ran over my bag which made the time even more memorable for me! The next day I was able to take a friend to visit that class in the Kali Mandir slum area. He is one of the chief supporters of my work. In Kali Mandir area the dwellings are very tiny and some "houses" are narrower than your outstretched arms.

We went to the "classroom" where some young boys were very keen to demonstrate the dance for us that they were going to perform on Independence Day (August 15th). The very small room was congested with the dancers and watchers. Through precarious feats of ingenuity they somehow avoided the ceiling fan, but it if had suddenly been switched on I envisioned decapitated young men all over the floor. These slum dwellers exude a zest for life that seems to be unknown anywhere else. The music was a crackling cacophony of screeches and bangs but they loved it, and although their style of dance wasn't exactly to our taste, we were amazed at their creativity.

Later we were standing beside a hoisted flag on the street next to the Kali Mandir (temple) when a procession of dancing children came by. The noise was terrific and the colours of their clothing and dancing matched it in exuberance. Of all Kolkata (apart from our visit to a vibrant church there), it was only here where we saw any form of celebration of the Independence of India 60 years ago. This was once known as a city of palaces, but is now a relic in motion—and one wonders why. Kolkata arrests all your senses, all your emotions, where the best and the worst happen at the same time.

The circumstances of the literacy students are by far the most tragic in Kolkata, and classes are held in some very inhospitable environments. The heat and the smell, and the "thick", motionless, heavy air is suffocating. One class was made up of young Muslim women from what is known as "Monkey Bazaar". These women collect coal for a living. They go from one street tea shop to the next where the leftover ash heap from cooking fuel has been dumped onto the street. They haul huge piles of it back home where they sieve through it with their hands and pick out the tiny remains of coal. They wash this and re-sell it. The men each keep a monkey which is usually tied on a chain to the wall. When the men are not breathing in drugs (as I have watched them doing) they go with their monkeys and have them perform tricks for money. It is sickening to see these monkeys.

One girl in the class was really ill so the teacher had the whole class pray for her. All laid hands on her while she fervently called on the name of the Lord Jesus for healing. They were all fully involved.

When I was leaving Kolkata, the taxi I was in stopped at some red traffic lights, and a man with mutilated arms approached me. He was trying to sell strings of Jasmine. These had a wonderful scent—far more potent than the European variety. I turned down the window and was looking for the money in the dark. Suddenly the lights turned to green and the taxi sped off before I could pay. He was running, trying to catch up but to no avail and only afterwards did I notice that he had laid many strings over the window. Here was I gaining something from a poor man granting me my favourite flower, Jasmine, at his great loss. This troubled me all the way home.

The vibrant church that I mentioned above had developed out of the many hundreds of children who had been rescued from Howrah Railway Station and many other parts of Kolkata by the Christian workers of Immanuel Ministries. This work had started in the late 1970s and early 1980s and continues to the present day. The work had just begun when I was involved with OM in Kolkata all those years ago. These children had grown up, overflowing with the joy of the Lord Jesus. Some of them have become my literacy teachers. One young man, Meetun, told me his story. I decided to write it in the form of a poem:

Meetun's story.

He came in fear and trembling.

Was it to some deathly clinic?

Would he find a wound on his body this time tomorrow?

An organ removed perhaps, or some other hideous calamity?

Would he once more be abused and beaten?

Instead of bread, would he again receive boiling oil

Poured onto his outstretched hand?

Who was this man?

Was it a trick … The police in disguise

Doing to him what they had done to the other boys?

Was it another clean-up of the station?

Like poisonous chemicals illegally dumped,

Was he also going to be deposited in the mangroves,

To be left as prey for the tigers of the Sunderbans?

Should he trust this man?

For he had never trusted anyone before.

It's hard to know when you're only seven.

Again the man came

Again he was invited—to dare to reach out beyond his present world,

To reach for the stars.

Maybe this time he would go.

He came in fear and trembling.

But then he noticed other boys there—

Once inmates of Howrah station like himself.

Now clean like the "good" children

Who rode the trains with their parents.

He too was about to become such a one.

He came and found something else.

Something that changed his life forever.

After a very short break back home in our town in Uttarakhand State, I was on the road again; this time to a small Himalayan lakeside town called **Bhimtal**. John took me in our car and it was a trip not without adventure. Bhimtal is between 400 and 500 kilometres from where we live.

The traffic between our town and Kashipur was hazardous to say the least, and in the evening the blinding lights affected our vision. We had several near-fatal accidents, so I'm glad we didn't often travel in our tiny car. We decided to stop for the night in a rather posh looking hotel where we even had air conditioning.

During the night the rain was extremely loud, and I kept wondering about this because the windows were closed. In the morning John opened the room door and, lo and behold—there was a river flowing through the hotel! A very grandiose curving stairway led from the lobby to the top floor. On this a waterfall was now cascading and spilling off the sides like a water feature in a shopping mall. We paddled down to the lobby where the water was pretty deep. But the most amazing thing for us was that the employees were just standing around as if nothing had happened. There were two upholstered sofas taking the full force of the water. Why had nobody moved them at the start? These are the great mysteries for the non-Indian mind.

Back on the highway, we wondered why there was no traffic and we soon discovered the reason. So many rivers had burst their banks and overflowed that now the roads themselves had become rivers.

When we finally got through all this and up into the mountains, we found that the incessant rain had caused many landslides reducing parts of the roads to narrow shifting tracks.

We finally arrived unscathed, and I had to begin the Teacher Training Workshop immediately (five hours late). The three-day training went well except for one young man who couldn't grasp the idea. The students at the mini Bible School in Bhimtal are usually very new in the faith. They come from remote villages and are especially poor, very religious and have minimal education.

I have been told that in every group of new students several are demon possessed. One young woman was unable to participate at all. She was very withdrawn. She appeared to be demented, and her friends said that she became like this quite suddenly. She used to be an average happy-go-lucky village girl. Now she growled like an animal and cried out in a voice other than her own. So they brought her to Bhimtal in the hope that she would get free as the others have done. This place seemed to me to be more like a spiritual midway-home than a Bible School where people came to get released; not from drugs but from Hinduism. Many have ruined minds, but after one year they are totally free, I'm told.

We celebrated my birthday with the students and staff as it fell on the final day. I could tell that they had never enjoyed such nice things to eat before, so it was an especially happy event.

John remained at the Bible School in Bhimtal for another week to teach from the Bible. I left and continued along that mountain road in a "share taxi" in the torrential rain only to get stuck on a landslide. I was on the way to villages near the Nepal border to encourage the classes of the trainees I taught last March.

10

Light or Dark—written on October 22nd, 2010

A typical day had passed. The monsoon had finished a month earlier but had been followed by some random, almost cyclonic storms. John was away in West Bengal and, as the evenings were lonely, I determined to go to the Bible study about six or seven miles away. We had had no electricity for two days so it was good to get out in the evening. It was already dark and the worst part of a storm was under way when I went to open the gates to get the car out. The wind pushed the gates in the opposite direction, and my left hand index finger got squeezed between them. Interesting to note what language the epithet came out in at that moment: German!

Whether it was due to the pain or that I had a sudden anointing of the Lord, I don't know, but my perception of the discussion which evolved during the Bible study was markedly sharp and clear. There was a big debate as to whether we should accept and eat food which had been offered to idols (*prasaad*)—a very real situation here. At least half the people admitted to accepting and eating it because they didn't want to cause offence. Two

41

men called it their weakness and those very two were full- time Gospel workers who admitted to finding it very difficult to share the Gospel!

At that moment I couldn't remember where the verses were which I wanted to read out but my Bible fell open exactly at that place (1 Corinthians 10: 19-29). If the food has clearly been sacrificed to idols and we know it, it is an offering to demons. We are told that we would be having a part at the table of demons if we choose to eat it. I could share what God had put on my heart. I have experienced that as soon as we compromise our faith we lose the respect of the people we try to reach and it was this very lack of respect that these men were bemoaning.

My problem was not *prasaad* but that I felt cut off from the world (perhaps in more ways than one). I could hardly find the Bible study house as it was in a new location. On the way home, the blinding lights of other cars were, as always, nightmarish. Drivers here either use every light they've got or no lights at all. Every driver has to have a driving licence because that's what the civilised world has, after all. But in India this has no relation to the ability to drive because you can purchase a licence from the Police.

The week before, a young biker came swerving down the road and crashed right into our car as John was driving. It was entirely the biker's fault. A hundred or so people gathered including the police and it ended up with John having to pay the biker 1,000 rupees (a lot here).

When I did get home after the Bible study the neighbourhood was totally blacked out. There was no one living in the downstairs apartment of the two storey house that we were renting at that time. There was no light, my phone battery was dead, my computer battery was dead, and the emergency lamp needed recharging. When I got inside I just had a few bent candles to write by.

Before leaving the Bible study one of the *prasaad*-eating men had thanked me and said how awesome it was that God gave His Word just at the right time. I agreed with him.

God has given us light in many areas of life so we can't pretend to be in darkness when the light is so obviously bright. But when it is dark there's nothing we can do but wait for God to give us His light at the right time.

As I meditated on this the storm returned in full force. The downstairs apartment's windows were banging and trees were swaying violently. But God's still small voice is louder than the storm if we are prepared to listen. I was reminded that Jesus actually talked to the wind when He rebuked it.

11

Discouraged in Dimapur—
written on November 5th, 2010

This last Friday was for me the lowest point that I reached in all the time we have been here in India. It also happened to be the day our daughter left and returned to Switzerland after being with us for several months. Although that would be a good enough reason to feel low, there was another.

John and I have just spent about a week in Kohima—the capital of Nagaland (the most easterly state of India) at the home of our daughter's fiancé's parents. This, as you can imagine, would be a story in itself—throwing our emotions all over the place. But the difficulty I'm facing is all to do with literacy.

I am ultimately here in the North-East region because I had been requested to give a Teacher Training Workshop in Ziro for the Apatani people of Arunachal Pradesh. This state borders China, and I am told China includes it on their maps as does India. It is high in the Himalayas, and is closed off in many ways to the rest of India.

In May 2009, as I explained previously, my co-worker and I had joined up with a group of local young believers of Apatani speakers to construct the primer in this language. One of the team members called Tada is also translating the New Testament. Tada and I have worked together for almost one-and-half years on all the details of the primer. He and the team have asked me time and again to come and teach. There would be the possibility to go to that area providing I would not be the only foreigner and providing we had the expensive permit required. So I said that, as soon as the book was printed, I would surely come, for without the books we couldn't do the training. A few months ago Tada had arranged everything for 8th, 9th and 10th November as that's when the rice would have been harvested, and the people would be free to come.

Thanks to the Desk Top Publisher used by my organisation we were able to finish the work in June. I pushed very hard for the publishers in Mangalore to get it printed and sent off in time. I was worried that everything would be done at the last minute.

Here in the North-Eastern states our mobile phone connections are automatically cut off due to a great deal of unrest in these regions. However, I was able to use someone's phone and contact Tada several times that week.

"Yes," he said, "all is arranged and they are expecting you, but the books have still not arrived!"

"Why not?" I asked.

"Because Mr. X has them in Guwahati (Assam). He will only come on November 11th with Mr. D (director of the publishers), and says he will only bring three copies to inaugurate the book on 13th."(I had asked for 1,000 books to be sent.)

"But Tada, you said you arranged everything including an inauguration on November 7th!"

"Yes, but he has changed all that," he replied.

"Well, when did you get to know he changed everything?"

"Just now!"

The usual prising out of information went on and on and Tada sounded very discouraged. I managed to get Mr. X's number and called him. Before I could speak he was yelling at me that he would have his inauguration on November 13th. I tried to make him understand that that was not my concern and he could have it whenever he wished, but that the training was all arranged for before that date. So I asked him if he would send the books (which he was withholding) up to Dimapur (a few hours further up the train line) where we could receive them and take them ourselves.

"No, no no!" he punched out. "We will give the training, you go home! We don't need you!" Yet I knew that only either my co-worker or I could do the training.

The man was extremely rude, in a frenzy and totally unreasonable. And I had no idea why. The shock left me shaking, and I could hardly dial Tada's number. I asked Tada if this Mr. X had been bypassed when he had made the arrangements. No, it had all been discussed with him.

To add to the mess, the permits we needed to enter Arunachal Pradesh (which were now officially available to tourists) had still not been granted in order for John and I to leave on Saturday 6th evening by night bus. So we had to cancel those bus tickets. We had applied for the permits about two months before. Officials had found out that we were Christians, and so they rejected us.

Now Tada was trying to find another way. Just when we needed the government's help so badly, all government offices closed down for two days for Diwali celebrations. Tada then told us to come on Monday 8th evening arriving Tuesday. He would come to the border with the permits himself. As we were about to purchase the bus tickets for Monday we were told that there would be a *bandh* (transport strike) that day so there would be no way we could leave Dimapur. Now everything was set for us to go on Tuesday night.

Tada phoned Mr. X and was told that there wouldn't be any training, that he would not bring the books, and that there would be training in July next year.

I asked myself, "Are we mad? Are we fools? Why have we decided to go there if this self-made boss doesn't want me?" One thing I knew was that all those expecting me would be discouraged if we didn't go. They might even have thought that we were not interested in them or that I had decided to leave them in the lurch. They already thought that it had been too long since we had first constructed the primer.

This Apatani tribe is a remote and very much unreached people. Most worship the sun and moon and their women have very disfiguring tattoos and blocks of wood in their noses to keep evil spirits away from them. It seems that EVERYTHING is against them from hearing or reading the Word of God.

12

We enter Arunachal Pradesh— written in November 2010

The day before John and I left Dimapur in Nagaland there had been an attack on a bus in the region that we would be going through. This is a frequent problem in volatile Assam. The insurgents took out the people from the bus and killed 15 of them and killed others in the bazaar. But we had no problems in our bus other than the ten-hour ride during which we were packed in and surrounded by other people's luggage up to our shoulders with everyone walking all over it.

We arrived at the Arunachal Pradesh border at 4am and were relieved to meet Tada who was waiting for us with the permits. How he finally managed to get us those permits I had no idea. After waiting one or two hours for them to be "passed", we got a taxi to Ziro, which took about five hours.

Tada and his wife Sheela have a "Hansel and Gretel" house in a bamboo forest. It was so good to see her again as it had been one-and-a-half years since we had done the primer construction.

Dimapur had been hot and humid (30° plus) and in Ziro the weather was about 16° at the hottest time of day. We had barely taken our "bath" (with a bucket full of water and a mug) when it seemed as if the whole of the Apatani Baptist Association was at the door. We were introduced to all the various leaders of the church. They welcomed us very warmly and repeatedly told us how glad they were that we had come. They arranged for us to go sight-seeing the next day. I was to start teacher training the day after. There was no way they were going to let us come all this way without that happening! The sight-seeing meant visiting one village after another of the Apatani tribe. There were about ten villages and nine Baptist churches.

The very first church in Apatani land of any denomination, known as Town Baptist church, was founded in Ziro in 1984, and the very first Apatani convert (in the mid-1970s) was Dr. Bamin Tada. There are about 50 to 60,000 Apatani and about 10,000 of them are Christian. The religion of the majority is called Donnyi Polo, (Donnyi meaning Sun—female and Polo or Poli meaning Moon—male).This is an animistic and shamanic religion where the followers are nature worshippers with the sun as their supreme deity.

We went in a house where little chicks were being sacrificed. This was being done in order to see the future or fortune of this family. While still alive, the chicks' livers were removed and the priests examined them to see what luck was in store for the family. All the relatives had come and were drinking rice beer. We learned a lot about these animistic rituals during this time. It was very common to see chicken eggs strung together, hanging from bushes and trees outside of people's houses. Sometimes we saw the enormous horns of a mithun wedged between the branches. A mithun is a bovine and the ones we saw were wild with a very thick piebald coat.

The geography of Arunachal Pradesh is perhaps the most beautiful I have yet seen in India—it is truly pristine. Although we had no time to venture beyond the Apatani district, I knew that behind those magnificent hills and forests were the lakes and mountains of the high Himalaya.

The villages of the Apatani looked like a pile of sticks to me. They live in bamboo houses, make bamboo matting and even cook their eggs and chicken in a piece of bamboo, stopping up the end with leaves and cooking it in the open wood fire. Though these people are very poor you will never see beggars or layabouts as you see in mainland India. Food costs at least double the price in this state and no one can afford to buy fruit. They work very hard in the rice fields (especially the women), and they breed fish in the same fields where the rice is growing. To get around you must walk on the mud walls of the rice fields (which the women also make).

The people who were coming for the training included four who had helped in the construction of the primer. I had to disappoint them by telling them that the books had got "stuck" in Guwahati but that they should pray for them to come soon.

The next day was the inauguration of the book with Mr. X who had turned up the night before. There was no time to talk with these people before the inauguration began. The people present consisted of many of those we had already met two days before.

Mr. D from the publishers spoke very well on church leadership, and Mr. X spoke about a past project and how this book will be useful for the next project. I had no idea what he was talking about.

And then I said a few words—just expressing my delight at seeing the book (albeit only one of each volume), and that I hoped for all the Apatani to become literate.

Then Sheela was asked to speak as the representative of the Apatani. She REALLY took the stage as she pleaded openly, without inhibition, for Mr. X to send up the books immediately. She told him, "Just last night I had a call from someone, telling me that in Hong village 20 people are waiting to learn to read and write, and when are we ever going to start?" She quoted several other similar pleas and requests and made it crystal clear how urgent the need was. She made her point and scored a "bull's eye" as far as I was concerned. After a meal that evening in Tada and Sheela's house, to which everyone was invited, I was left feeling that the situation had been taken care of without me having to say or do anything. The next day Mr. X left.

Curiously, that evening we were told that a parcel of books was in the office. Tada collected it and to our delight 150 primers (Book 1) were in it! Whether Mr. X had had second thoughts, whether it was Mr. D's idea, or that someone else had urged them to bring these books, I have no idea. But there they were!

The next day the teacher training continued and, to their great surprise, I could hand each of the twelve trainees a book. The participants were very bright and quick to catch our organisation's signature method. Each trained person expected to start a class in the immediate future. If each had an average of ten learners this meant that there would be just enough books for the time being.

We had to leave the day after the training was over as our train tickets had been booked so that we would catch one from Guwahati in Assam.

How I praise and thank God who stood there for me. I didn't need to have a confrontation with Mr X. I had no need to defend myself—others did it for me. They had made everything very clear on my behalf, so to speak.

We left Ziro in a jeep for the border town of Nahalagun. What a surprise we had when the "rest" of the Apatani Baptist organisation met us and had cooked food for us. The secretary of the whole organisation was thrilled that the training had taken place.

Another man was standing at the gate to welcome us. It was Dr. Bamin Tada—the very first Apatani convert. He is also a very senior medical doctor. He is famed in India as a TB (tuberculosis) specialist. He has worked a lot for the World Health Organisation, speaking in Geneva and elsewhere. Though he didn't say it, it was due to his untiring work that TB has been reduced by half in Arunachal Pradesh, and the state has one of the lowest incidences of the disease in all of India. We were so humbled to be met by this man, and he was delighted about literacy for his people.

From our arrival to our departure the Apatani did not cease to speak of the love of God and the change that Christ had brought in their lives.

13

The Ironic Peace of Kandhmal—written March in 2011

Odisha is a large state on the eastern coast of India's Bay of Bengal. Compared to the more tropical climate of West Bengal, Odisha is much drier and hotter, though you will still find coconut palms on most of the plains. In the dry season, which lasts about eight or nine months of the year, there is too little water to grow much variety of cereal, so the fields lie in wait for the rains when paddy is planted. However, you will see mile after mile of cashew nut groves. These trees are large and sprawling.

The thing I love about Odisha's topography is the many pools it boasts. These are mostly natural mini lakes dotted all over the countryside and you even find them in the cities. A typical Indian scene is to see people at the steps of such a pool taking their bath or washing their clothes. It has changed little since when I first came here in 1980. Odisha has a population of 40 million and most of the people live on the coastal plains.

It took seven hours to drive from Bhubaneswar to where I am staying in Kandhmal. The tribal zone begins with the abrupt change in landscape as we ascend into the beautiful, forested hills.

Tranquil alpine valleys meet the eye. The rich, red soil remains the same however, and is for me Odisha's giveaway hallmark. The hills lie north-south throughout western Odisha. There are 62 tribes belonging to three ethnic groups, and they make up 24 per cent of the state's population. These aboriginal tribes are known as Adivasis. As much as 16 per cent of them comprise of Dalits, the lowest in the caste system.

The people were probably driven here by the Aryan invaders; the forests are unsuitable for cultivation except for the turmeric root from which the yellow spice powder, or *haldi* as it is known here, is obtained. It is said that the best turmeric of all India is from here. Tobacco also grows like weeds everywhere.

Kandhmal is a district divided into twelve "blocks". *Mal* means hills and Kandh or Kondh is the name of the tribe. I am in Daring Bari, a town in the only block where the people were not persecuted two years ago. This is because 90 per cent of the inhabitants are Christians; so, as they were in the majority, they were left alone by their neighbours. However, I am told not to stay more than four or five days as things could change. Naxalites are also rampant here and, as I write, the search is on for a government minister who was kidnapped from Bhubaneswar a couple of days ago and is possibly somewhere close by.

In this block live about 200,000 people yet the area appears to be scarcely populated. The Kondh speak Kui which is a Dravidian language. The tribe is sub-divided. There is Desai Kondh, Dongaria Kondh, Kutia Kondh ... in fact there are 58 sub-divisions with many dialects. So you can imagine what a difficult task it is to help tribal people become literate and I am talking about just one tribe!

The house where the literacy teacher training is being held has been rented out to us by a man who had to flee his home two years ago from another block. He and his family lost everything they had. The same goes for Paul, the man who invited me here and who once attended our institute in 2007. Being pastors and church leaders they are marked men and can never return to their homes which were burned or razed to the ground, or to their land which was their sole source of support.

Paul described to me how the attacks began for him in 2008:

They (Hindu extremists) came and the first thing they did was to desecrate the churches—mostly by burning. Then they burned all the Christians' homes down. At midnight he, his wife and small son fled, escaping into the forest. They walked and climbed for five days and nights. They had no food, and so he attempted to buy some from shopkeepers by leaving the cover of the forest and going into a town. But as soon as they realised he was a Christian food was denied. They had to cross a river, chest deep and could not swim. Twice during this time tigers passed by them. Paul said the tigers came so close, obviously aware of their presence, but never looked up at them and just quietly walked passed! He said in those moments he remembered Daniel in the lion's den and claimed the same protection. The Lord was merciful and answered their prayers. He said to me, "Just imagine—an enormous tiger walking peacefully by yet, at the same time, Oriyans were committing brutal acts of murder, rape and violence to their own people!" Something very, very sick was in the minds of these people.

All that happened in 2008. Yet today thousands of Christians are still living in tents as they have nowhere to go.

I made it to this area of Kandhmal with 700 copies of the primer which we constructed in 2009. This teacher training has been hard work, mostly because of the translation needed. Paul and others translated for me from Hindi into Kui and we were using Oriya books. This begs the question, why didn't we write the primer in Kui? Well, there are one million Kui speakers and, as I already said, over 40 million Oriya speakers. The Oriya has to come first so we can reach out all over the state; it is also the trading language between the tribal people. They have asked me to come and write one in Kui later this year—let's see.

The participants were shy. As always with trainees all over India, when they made their word cards as samples for future lessons, they struggled tremendously. The average Indian has no idea how to measure with a ruler. This may come as a surprise to the reader, but I have the same experience every time. They do not know the difference between inches and centimetres. They cannot measure anything, they cannot draw a straight line using a ruler, and they cannot use scissors and prefer to tear everything! This is for me a great test of patience. Let me construct a primer in some strange language but as for Teacher Training Workshops—I need "kilos" of endurance.

Removing their timidity and turning them into literacy tutors is no small task. But when they've got through it successfully and can demonstrate a lesson before us all, their joy has no limits; and if they all make it, my joy has no limits.

After the training period was over, we went to start some classes—or so I thought. I imagined myself finally being able to sit back and watch classes run. Instead each turned out to be an inauguration ceremony in various churches where I was the speaker. In fact, on one day it was a women's revival meeting ending in an inauguration ceremony. Again I was the speaker (the only one), and I had to "open the Word of God to them for not less than an hour!" Me of all people!

On returning to Bhubaneswar I was pampered to bits by the very loving family of Pastor Sahu. Pastor Sahu had organised a Teacher Training Workshop for me with the goal of making the slum dwellers in his four churches literate. This training was simpler as Pastor Sahu knew Hindi well and, as the participants all spoke Oriya, the translation was straightforward.

One day the family decided I must be very tired so they put me on the family bed and Sahu's wife was showing her eight-year-old daughter how to massage my legs! But their cute little five-year-old son couldn't bear to be left out, so there was an argument about who had which limb to massage! Finally he got my left arm and leg and his sister got the right. I thought they would give up after a minute or two but no, it got pretty serious, and they amazingly dedicated themselves to the task and gave me a wonderful massage. I thought I should pretend to go to sleep to relieve them and so, sure enough, when they thought I was sleeping, they tip-toed out of the room!

One day we all went to Puri beach. I didn't think they would want to go in the sea as most Indians don't swim. However, it seemed like all Odisha was in the ocean and, after we had stood there knee deep in water screaming at every wave for a while, I couldn't resist it any longer and took off for a long dreamed of swim!

14

Prostitution in Pune—written in August 2011

Just over a year ago I had given literacy training to a group of Nepali migrants in Pune, but only one class was started in the Nepali church. The real passion of the people was to help the women in the red light area of Pune which I mentioned in an earlier chapter. Due to the enormous difficulties, nothing till now in the area of literacy has been started.

Rina has an amazing love for these people and that's why she opened a beauty salon as a means of contact with these women. It's her platform from which she can reach them. Over the years she has been able to build a relationship of trust, not only with the prostitutes but also with some of their "owners", the owners of brothels, and even the big "daddy" (Godfather) who "protects" them and who I bumped into when he came to collect his share of the profits. Officially in this area there are 6,000 women but it is obvious that there are far more than that.

The beauty salon or parlour is "where it's at" and the place to get to know these women. It couldn't be in a more central location as it is on the third floor of a grimy multi-storey and multi-purpose complex where scores of women position themselves in the street below, and would-be clients wander up and down like packs of pariah dogs, hungry for anything on offer. As Rina wrenched the bars of the elevator to one side and we stepped in, she pointed to the ever present rust-red spittle of *paan* all around the cubicle.

"We cleaned all of this but it didn't last a week," she told me.

We took the stairs the next time and every corner—in fact every free space along the walls of the complex—was covered in the stuff.

"We cleaned all of this too but look at it now! We have a few Indian N.G.O.'s on this floor. This one is M.S.M."

"What's M.S.M.?" I asked.

"Men sex with men"

I looked inside. There was an over-glamorous woman sat on the floor and a bold poster on the wall: "Sex isn't sin—use condoms."

Rina and Purnam (another woman I gave the training to last year) are both from Nepal. They are hard-working people who, although they have their own families to look after, also want to see transformation among these women. They have taken the risk of being grouped along with the sex workers. They will always be tainted simply by having Nepali faces and walking among the brothels. Yet the great paradox is that the Indian sex workers are considered holy!

Rina and Purnam told me that most of the Indian women of this area have been given over to the goddess Yellamma. This religious Hindu cult is keenly followed in Karnataka State. Whenever there are too many girls in a family, at least one will be given to the goddess for Kama Sutra practice. So in the name of religion the girl is sacrificed to "god's work" i.e. prostitution.

From then onwards she will always wear a special talisman around her neck and a good amount of gold jewellery. She is usually about 17 or 18 years of age but may also be much younger when given.

Sitting amongst the women outside the brothels repulsed me at first. Some had very sinister looks; some on the other hand seemed ordinary. Some looked really sick (we took one to the doctor), and a large number seemed mad.

Madness was the overwhelming feeling about the place. It was an open-air mental institution, or at least that was my first impression. The girls and women were of all ages; from about 17 years up into middle age. I think I was more shocked at seeing so many older ones. None were particularly pretty. All were very coarse.

The women live in groups and stick together but the groups do not intermingle. The animosity between them was almost tangible. One group was particularly grim. Rina said that depression often settles on them and they sit for hours without talking. It reminded me of the dogs here in India: packs of dogs, apparently in peace, lying near to each other one moment, and in the next, there is a huge fight for no obvious reason.

Another group surprised me because the women were friendly. One young woman (the only attractive one) had a little boy who had no real fingers or toes. He had been born that way, she said. We tried to cheer him up but he was very distraught and very anxious. Another older boy of about ten years held onto Rina. Later we took him back to the beauty salon along with another child for want of a better place to go. We fed them something and let them play with a teddy bear.

As we spent time with the friendly group they became inquisitive and wanted to know why I was there. This was my cue to explain the literacy programme. One by one they appeared to show genuine interest in learning to read. One woman was very keen. She said she wanted to be literate so that she could count her money. She wanted to understand how much she handed over to her boss each month. I found out that an average income was around Rs40,000 per month (about US$625—a large amount here). Of this, Rs20,000 goes straight to the boss. Then the woman pays a very high rent to the brothel owner. Then there are all the others like the Godfathers who want their slice of the cake. She is usually left with less than Rs5,000 to survive on. All the women wore very cheap clothing. For me this was a clear sign that they didn't have much.

So becoming literate would be no small thing. Such simple number work—a basic necessity—could prove dangerous for

Rina, Purnam and the women and, of course, be detrimental to the boss's business. A literacy class is to start next week; we have a list of around ten women.

Rina took me inside a brothel. Two steps ahead of me was a client. He hurriedly entered the adjoining room with a "worker" who looked like a washer-woman while we sat down in the depressing boss's quarters. Rina knew this boss well and I was told ahead of time that she wanted to give everything up and follow Jesus. Rina was sharing her faith with the boss for about ten minutes when the client reappeared. He wiped his brow with a handkerchief and left. A moment later a fierce looking man appeared with a huge moustache. He sat nervously waiting for Rina to finish so that he could collect some money. I found out later that that he was the area Godfather. The woman worker came out and there was a short discussion, and then he was gone. Several women were in the room now. I had memorised John 8:1–11 in Hindi and I asked if I could share this with them. I emphasised every detail of the woman's encounter with Jesus and His overwhelming compassion moved them. One woman began to weep. The boss said it would be too dangerous to become a Christian. What should she do? A pimp had threatened Rina with death already but the Lord had delivered her.

I asked Rina: "What about all the girl children that we hear about who are sold from Nepal?"

"Oh, they are deep inside the labyrinth of brothels, they never come out." She said she had managed to meet a 13-year-old. The girl had been an outgoing, carefree child from the mountains. Now she never speaks.

15

Jonathan—written between 2011 and 2015

Jonathan, who lives in south India, is one of several Nepali teachers I have trained. He did amazingly well, and started a class with seven students—six ladies and one young man—immediately after completing his training in 2011.

I was there when the class met for the first time. We all crowded into his very small, basic home, which he shared with his alcoholic stepfather.

Of course, the small children came along too, and the first evening was very chaotic (from my perspective) with yet other church members coming in to watch. There was a great sense of both achievement and euphoria on that first evening among both teachers as well as students. No one had believed that it was possible to learn to read so much in the very first lesson. After the Bible reading and explanation, one woman jumped to her feet and asked if she could share her testimony. She told a dramatic story of how Jesus had healed her after years of bleeding— just like in the story which had been read to her. She was really overcome with emotion, and we all could rejoice with her. Watching a class in action encouraged me so much.

Jonathan is a born teacher, and relates especially well to the group, yet his life has been far from plain sailing. He is mature, warm, thoughtful and kind. He's intelligent and speaks five languages fluently. He articulates his words with such clarity that it was no surprise when he was chosen from 150 applicants for the job as radio broadcaster and disc jockey for All India Radio. He's done a BA in Mass Communications and will continue his MA in Journalism. Being pretty huge physically, you wouldn't think of him as Nepali.

In 2011 he was just getting over the death of his mother who had died in great suffering the previous year. It was this suffering which caused him so much anguish. They had already shared so much pain together and had always been there for each other. It was her great wish to see her son "well settled" job-wise and financially, but she died without seeing anything. He told me that he loved her so much.

Some years before that there had been another wave of pain. His little seven-year-old sister had had a cancerous tumour in her leg and had to have the whole leg amputated. They were just learning to cope with that when she developed lung cancer. She died in 2005 aged ten years. He has no other siblings.

Prior to that was the first wave of heartache when he lost his father, also to cancer, when he was only nine-years-old in 2000.

When I talked with him he seemed far older than his 20 years. He is very outgoing and appears to have a strong sanguine personality. He is also very sensitive to the needs of others. He cooks all the main meals for his grandmother who lives in the neighbourhood with another family, as well as doing so much for the Nepali church in Bangalore.

I met Jonathan again a year later. I found him propped up on the sofa-bed. He had been on the back of his motorbike while his friend was driving it. They had just purchased some food, and as they drove off a truck came at high speed and hit them. The friend was not hurt but Jonathan sustained a broken leg. Being so traumatized at seeing all his family members leave hospital dead, he refused to go to one to have his leg put in plaster. He literally lay on his bed for months until it healed by itself. During this time he, not surprisingly, became very depressed. His moods changed suddenly and he thought he was going mad.

A few more years down the road have elapsed since then. Jonathan has opened his life story to me more and more. Before his father died the family had been doing well with a family-run restaurant. They had a very smart house with servants. But between the ages of four to 12 he was repeatedly raped by the male servants. This is the reason, he says, that he cannot have a girlfriend. Psychologically he cannot associate the idea of a sexual partner with someone of the opposite sex. He has girls as friends and many are attracted to him, but he cannot ever imagine being in love or getting married. If anything, he is attracted to men, a fact which he abhors about himself. When he is depressed he hates his life and, since each of his family members died five years apart from each other, he was sure his turn would come by the time of his birthday in 2015.

However, he has one primary passion and that is FOOD and cooking! He applied to several top colleges to train as a chef. After several setbacks he was finally accepted in a reputable college in

South India. Though he had had a very good job working for Google, he left it and is now very happy learning the fine art of culinary creation. This, I do believe, is a major turning point in his life. His birthday has been and gone, and he has passed over a great hurdle in his life.

16

A Day in Church— written in September 2011

Today I physically did next-to-nothing, yet today was a day I got to know God a little better.

The church we went to this morning was one of those low on my list of churches to go to. That's not because I had any resentments or negative feelings towards anyone from that church; on the contrary, I have a lot of respect for Surendran the Tamil pastor. He is a godly man, and he is also very knowledgeable. He helped me when I was writing the Tamil primer. But the services are always dreary and few seem motivated. Surendran always seems like a one-man-band. He entertains us with some good and also with some very dull songs, the microphone is bad and everything sounds very muffled.

When we arrived he was saying something about the power of God and how we also should have the power as the early Christians had, etc. etc. The old cynic in me surfaced. The negative came up … Yeah, yeah … how many times am I to hear that … etc. (having an off day?) We'll sing a few songs and attempt to lift ourselves up a rung or two and should we imagine after two hours that we now live in the power of the resurrection?!

When the lay preacher, who had also come that day, fired out his sermon in the "I know you're not listening" style (in other words – he was shouting his head off), I started relating more to my phone, something I never normally do in church! Just as I was doing this a voice at the back of the small hall began an incessant "aaaah" in the loudest, most uncanny tone I had ever heard in my life. It was a young man in his twenties who continued his desperate crying.

"Why doesn't the preacher shut up and go and see?" I kept thinking. I started trembling and felt weird. Thankfully a few of the older men got up and went to him. However, his screaming would not stop. I could see him shaking violently. This went on throughout the sermon making it impossible to hear anything intelligible, not to mention the muffling microphone.

I think Surendran had retired to his apartment during the sermon and maybe didn't know what was going on. But, at the end of the service, he reappeared and went to the man. He spent time there with him, and then took him by the hand and brought him to the front. The man again started his heart-rending "aaaah". It was evident that had he had a bad pain, he would not have such strength to shout like that. It didn't appear to be a physical problem. The loudness and intensity of his voice made me think that had he pushed against the wall, he would have brought it down easily. He fell to the floor, and the violence of his shaking was throwing him about. He had two bewildered friends standing by watching as well as members of the congregation.

Surprisingly for me not everyone was amazed at this spectacle, and some were even at the rear of the hall chatting and drinking tea. I could not bring myself to stand drinking tea when this poor fellow seemed in such agony. I started praying fervently for him. Then I noticed others were doing the same. The guy was soaked through in sweat. Surendran was talking to him, not trying to reason with him but telling him something in a controlled and quiet voice. At first the man got worse, and then he lay on his back and seemed to sleep. Then he sat up and Surendran gave him a glass of water. He took this in a perfectly normal way. Then he sat on a bench and the whole thing started again. Surendran was quietly rebuking the evil spirit which possessed him, and finally I heard him say a little louder "Go, get out and be gone". This evil spirit again made the man jolt and jerk in a horrible way, and then suddenly he became very calm and peaceful. He looked very tired but otherwise normal. He and his friends were directed to Surendran's apartment. I asked Surendran if they had come for the first time and he replied "Yes". I had noticed they were all wearing red threads around their wrists—a typical Hindu thing.

The power of God overcame the Evil One in that man's life, and I do believe he was delivered. I felt so ashamed of my cynicism once again. I praised God for His goodness and love for all people.

The presence of God outside of space and time filled my thoughts. How would anyone want to worship a lesser god? Our God is the Creator of the whole universe, and yet at the same time loves us rebellious, foolish, conceited humans. It is no use asking "why" … that's the character of God.

17

Primer Construction for the Kui—written in December 2011

We had been to Europe for three months, and almost as soon as we arrived back in India we were on the road again: John to West Bengal for Bible teaching and me to Odisha. This time I was going to do the Kui primer construction. I really can't stop praising God for how well it went. This was the first time I had done a primer alone without any other facilitator to work with.

Primer construction is really hard work and very demanding. You have to have your wits about you concerning every action the team is undertaking. I had organised the team into two groups producing stories with limited letters per lesson. Then the procedure is that when I've checked each story, letter for letter in a language I barely comprehend (in this case Kui), and in a script that I'm not over familiar with, I have to write it down, and then break all the new words into syllables in the right places, and write them in the template boxes. So I need to become familiar with the consonant and vowel patterns, and make sure they are right for a potential reader to learn from. The typist writes up my work, and on we go—in this case for 92 lessons.

The Kui people only have the Bible and a Christian song book in their language. Their grammar has not been documented and there is no dictionary. It belongs to the Dravidian language family. We used the Oriya script which, fortunately, I could recall a lot of having done the Oriya primer in 2009.

I had been asked to do this primer by Paul. He was one of many who had his house burnt down (twice) during the persecution: once at Christmas 2007 and then again in 2008. Several months earlier, he had phoned me to say that he had been diagnosed with a brain tumour. Nevertheless he insisted that he should come and help the team in the work. He had changed the venue three times; the second choice "P" was struck off the list because it was on "high alert". "P" had been at the epicentre of the persecution. So, when I was on the way to the airport feeling relieved to be going to Gopalpur, Paul phoned to say it was going to be in "P" after all!

Detour

Just before leaving for Odisha to do this primer construction, I got a call from Kingfisher Airlines to say that all my flights had been cancelled. I spent the rest of that day arranging new flights. But now they were sending me all over the map via Kolkata to get to Bhubaneswar. The main concern was that I would arrive late in Kolkata, and the connecting flight was the following morning at 7am.

On arrival in Kolkata my heart sank when I saw the dingy, miniscule airport. There was nowhere to lie down. I collected my luggage, and followed the sign for "airport manager". While talking to him or whoever it was sitting under the sign, he said there were dormitories for Rs700 in the airport, but the peon's nod quickly told him there wasn't. The peon took me over to the Kingfisher boss. He was sitting in his cubicle dripping in gold finger rings. He came out and amazed me with his pleasant manner. He got me a hotel room and said I wouldn't have to pay. Wow! He was efficient as well! He popped back into his cubicle, and then out again, and asked if I would be wanting dinner?

"No", I replied as it was way past midnight—just a bottle of water. But was the hotel nearby? Well not exactly … He queued at the pre-paid taxi stand for me, got me my taxi, and told me that tomorrow's return taxi fare would be reimbursed. I was given a voucher for a certain hotel. He said it was about half-an-hour away or a little more, and then asked whether I would be wanting breakfast in the morning?

"No, not at 5am", I replied. I had to be back at the airport by 5:45am.

I marvelled at the low level, no–star hotel because it was clean and most things worked! At 5:15am I was up and heading back to the airport. The driver must have been told to rush as he was careering down the highway. Then he turned round to have a discussion about the fare. Well, I thought, I will get reimbursed at the airport anyway. I told him to switch the meter on. It ran into thousands within minutes. The Indian Ambassador taxi was flying down the road when we suddenly hit a wall of fog. I yelled for him to slow down (politely) but when he didn't, I yelled again (not politely), and we just missed smashing into a car in front. He slowed down to try and free up the windscreen wipers with one hand as they wouldn't work. I said that that wouldn't help anyway, but he kept trying. The car slowed right down to a halt as if there was no more petrol. Now the car had broken down. The driver was cursing all the while. He was busy out in the fog under the bonnet calling his helper to bring the matches. "Oh no!" I wondered if he knew what he was doing. As he lit a match he told his helper to start the engine. I was about to eject myself from the back, but anyhow the car still didn't react. Now I was sure to have missed the plane. (This wouldn't be the first time from this airport.) It was 6am and I knew that they stopped you from going through to security well in advance. Finally the car cranked up again, and coughing and spluttering into motion, we idled along as the driver cursed our way to the airport. So we finally arrived.

"How much?" I asked. I was dreading the answer—there was no time to argue, and definitely no time to get reimbursed.

"Two hundred and fifty rupees, and give me an extra fifty for all my trouble". I was delighted. I grabbed my bags out of the back and ran into the airport. Crowds, no hordes of people were queuing up to put their luggage through the X-ray. I skipped the crowd, waving my ticket, and was able to go to the front and put mine straight through the X-ray. On to the check-in. My stuff was three kilos overweight, but as the plane was about to go, they waived me on. On to security: there must have been 500 people in the snake-like queue extending well into the departure lounge. Five planes were boarding, and mine was at the top of the list with red and green lights flashing.

The Kingfisher man said, "Just go, go past them all." But as I ducked under one band after another, I heard complaints, and I was stopped by a security guard. Then, for some reason, the man at the conveyor belt beckoned me to come to the front. I managed to get my net-book and bag onto the X-ray, shoes off, shoes on, battled through all the label stamping, ran to the gate, into the bus, onto the plane and off!

I spent two days in Bhubaneswar, and managed to visit some of the classes that were started nine months earlier in March. After this it was on to "P". Once again I found myself in the prettiest place in all India. I think I say that everywhere I go because the Indian geography is so varied and wonderful. The rural areas are unspoilt by man, which is why they are so attractive to me.

There were ten of us working on the primer for the first few days. Janga, a Nepali contact who has helped me in the past, came to give a hand on the computer side. We didn't know what our computer member of the team was going to be like, and as I had expected, he didn't know too much so Janga's help was invaluable. I had no time to spend on such matters. On December 13th Janga had to leave for his engagement ceremony in Nepal.

Paul did his utmost to help; he managed to give a lot of input for the first few days, but the pain he was suffering increased as time went on. This troubled me a lot. On some days he was feeling too ill to come. His nephew, also a member of the team, would bring him each day, and take him home again. The rest of us stayed on the compound eight kilometres outside "P" town.

I thoroughly enjoyed working with the Kui people. They were so patient and gentle. They found the task very difficult at the beginning but they worked so hard. When Janga had left, and Paul and his nephew didn't turn up, I wondered how I would manage as they didn't know much Hindi, and the typist using the computer was not very confident. I was worried that they would all get discouraged, and wondered if I would be able to hold the team together. But praise God, they all seemed to change into the next gear, stepping up their efforts, and took it upon themselves to see this primer through. It was great to observe this sense of responsibility in each of them. There was more to them than I first thought.

Each morning we started the day with singing and morning devotion. I asked a different member to share something from his or her life. One day it was Santona's turn. I couldn't understand most of what she said but realised it was very serious from the way she cried. These were not sobs of self-pity. I had the idea to get Tiki, the Hindu Brahmin girl who worked on the compound, to translate her story for me as I gathered it was about the persecution. I have shared her story in the following chapter.

I shared my sleeping quarters with two rats, one black one and the other brown. The room itself was very clean, and I think these were rural rats, and were just curious to know what was on the other side of the wall. When I shooed them they would run back out through the vent high up in the wall. However one night a mouse gave me no end of trouble and I got no sleep. It ran and jumped all over the place including the bed and, as there was no electricity, it was really freaky having a mouse jump on me in the dark. A skinny guy on the compound had been appointed as a security guard. He had been given a uniform and a gun (but no bullets). He slept on the other side of my wall. So at 4am, when I couldn't stand it any longer, I called him in to get the mouse. He was somewhat perplexed as a mouse had never troubled anyone in his life's experience before, and he found it very funny. He beat about the room with a stick, but failed to catch it. The next day the whole team and others besides had discovered my weak point, and were full of smirks and smiles. The guys got together and blocked up the vent. The big joke was that if the security guard couldn't protect me from a mouse, how would I fare if a greater enemy came?

Midway through the primer construction we were visited by the police. They wanted to know everything so I obliged them with so much technical detail that it went over their heads. But then they took the primers in Oriya that I had done in the past and examined them. I must say I was feeling very apprehensive. The next day Paul came and told me that they had called at his house before coming to me. As his was a registered organisation he had nothing to hide. But we knew that trouble might come.

What happens every Christmas is a good example of the problems that the Kui face. "P" is a Hindu Oriya town. Each Christmas there is a strike in the town and the extreme Hindu party makes sure that neither public nor private transport is allowed to run between December 21st and 27th. This is so that Christians may not be able to get together for any celebrations. Most stores are closed so that there is nothing to buy at Christmas. It is a very tense time for the Kui.

18

Oh Odisha! Santona's Story

I wrote this down as Tiki, the Hindu Brahmin woman translated for me from the Kui language into Hindi while we sat on Santona's bed in the dark due to a power cut; I had a tiny torch.

Santona's father was a Hindu priest but had died before she was born. Her mother was a Hindu teacher. Santona was at that time teaching young children at the local school. In the village there were 55 households where the residents knew nothing about Jesus. A pastor was living in this village and was always preaching about Jesus Christ. He gave her a biography of someone's life to read, but she hated anything to do with Jesus. Still, he encouraged her to read it. While reading it her mother kept coming to try and stop her from doing so. What the book said about the heart of man rang true, and this began to disturb her. She went to discuss the book with the pastor and her mother followed her. Her mother decided the pastor must be a foreigner as he was spreading a foreign religion, though in fact, he was a Kui man. Santona managed to go to her aunt's house to meet and talk freely so that the pastor could explain things clearly. Her mother found out and was furious. The more she became interested in Jesus, the worse it got and her mother began to hate her, and told her to go to her grave like her father. She started reading the Bible in the middle of the night, but the family members caught her and a lot of quarrelling began.

She read Jesus' words, "The truth shall make you free." She prayed that she would know the truth, and that the true God should reveal himself. She had a dream or a vision in the night where Jesus was showing her the two choices she had in her life. He had her follow Him up a stream. When she told her family the next day they threw her out of the house.

She went to Bible College for some time, and then dared to return home. Her mother had a large and very deep wound on her left buttock—whether it was a bed sore or not I don't know, but she had been in horrible pain for some time. Santona offered to pray for healing, but her mother replied bitterly that there was no god to heal her. Santona said she would pray anyhow. Within a couple of days the wound was gone. This caused a huge stir in the family as the wound had been really deep. The whole family admitted that there was only one God. They were three sisters, three brothers, two sisters-in-law and her mother, and they all turned to Jesus Christ. Her eldest brother went to Bible College, and is presently in God's service.

In 2008 there was a *danga*—a riot or attack. A group came and broke down the church in a village close by. They went on to destroy two more churches. All the villagers went to the village head. They pleaded with him to do something and to tell the police. He retorted that they had only broken church buildings and none of their houses. It was August 25th— it was a Monday and it was 11am. Some of the group came and surrounded Santona's family's house.

I asked her, "About how many people?" expecting her to say nine or ten.

She said, "1,500". This had become clear later. The family were all on their knees praying, and hiding in the bathroom. Suddenly the attackers broke down the door. They were holding axes and knives, and all had coloured their faces with red paint. They first looted the place, after which they set the veranda and a motorbike on fire. Then they set the whole house on fire. The family were desperately trying to escape. The attackers began kicking one of her brothers and, in the most horrific way imaginable, they murdered him. Santona and one brother escaped through a hole in the roof. The others managed to escape but she didn't know where they were. She and her sister-in-law and four-month-old baby, whose father had just been slaughtered, fled to the jungle to hide. They stayed there three days and nights till eventually the police came shouting that they could come to safety.

In Raikia, where persecution had been very great, a relief camp was set up. Thousands of Christians went there and lived in tents, staying for two years. The Hindus would not allow them to return to their own villages, and had taken all their land. The hate was very real. After the two years another relief camp was set up in another town, and Santona has been living in a tent there till now. Yes—she and the other woman in my team are still living in tents.

19

Nepali Diaspora, Sharp Minded and Focussed— written in May 2012

After a number of Teacher Training Workshops in Pune and elsewhere I went down to South India for further literacy celebrations. It was a great joy to return to the class where I had observed Jonathan begin his teaching. Within the record time of six months he had completed both volumes of the Nepali primer. One of the women had never held a pen or read a single letter in her life prior to this.

I gave them all a reading and writing test which included the writing of a letter to a pastor. Their letters were not only lengthy but also interesting to read. On the Sunday they all read a chapter or more from the Bible before the whole congregation. It was a very proud moment indeed, and it struck me that they were probably more fluent than the rest of the 100 or so members of the congregation. I presented them each with a completely new translation of the Nepali Bible—hot off the press. The teachers had good reason to feel proud, and they too got a Bible each. I am constantly amazed at these people. Many have gone through terrible hardships which western people would probably find hard to believe. They are true gems for Jesus. They will be amongst the shiniest people in heaven!

Soon after that I went to Sitarganj in North India to give a Teacher Training Workshop there. Sitarganj is still within our state but almost touches the border or the bottom left corner of Nepal. I took a sleeper class night train and got no sleep at all. The fan made us all freeze, and it wouldn't go off. As I was on the top bunk I got its full blessing as it was almost touching me. Everyone was mistaking the light switches for the fan, on-off, on-off, and people were getting on and off the train all night. For most of the passengers it had been turned into a loud family time, and no one could care less as to whether anyone was trying to sleep. I had to disembark at 5am. I had over 100 books as well as my own belongings for the next few weeks as I was going to Nepal afterwards. No one was in the mood to help me get all the stuff off the train, and I just managed to get it onto the platform before the train left again. Dragging everything to the exit was tricky— keeping your eye on one item while pulling the other to be sure it didn't get stolen. There were no rickshaws or buses or anything, and I still had a further trip of over an hour to get to Sitarganj. I waited an hour till it became daylight, and a helpful man got me an auto (three-wheel taxi) from somewhere. This took me to a "share taxi" which looked like a Land Rover. Fourteen of us squeezed in and we were soon on our way. An hour later the pastor found me and, soon afterwards, I got started.

The 13 participants were all capable, and learned the method well in the three day training. As Sunday was the next day, I decided to present the certificates in church. But on Saturday night I got really sick. That night I thought I wouldn't leave the town alive. I called John pleading with him to come as I thought I would never make it on the next lap of the journey. So he took the next night train, went through the same procedure and, after arriving, had to preach in the church, and present the certificates on my behalf. John phoned our daughter and son-in-law, who are both doctors, and they prescribed something. During the next few days I improved.

Two classes were ready to begin right away, and we were able to go out to the village and watch this happen. What idyllic villages! It was wheat harvest, and many in the area were *Sadarjis* (Sikh people) wearing their brightly coloured turbans—not the *fix fertig* ready-made turbans you see city people wearing. These were yards of the brightest cloth wound round their heads, making those bearded men look like Maharajas. Most of the learners, however, were Tharu, Hindu people. What an exciting challenge!

20

Janga's Wedding—
written in May 2012

From Sitarganj John and I left for Nepal via Lucknow to attend Janga's wedding. Janga, as I have previously mentioned, has been working among the Nepali diaspora in India. He has linked me up with many Nepali churches where I have given literacy training.

When we arrived in Nepalganj, Janga and his best friend Mehul from Delhi (who was to be his best man) came to meet us. Janga had only arrived the night before us! Dear Janga didn't even have a suit to wear so he spent the next two days getting one tailored in the very-basics-only town of Nepalganj. We enjoyed the fellowship of his church, and John preached on Good Friday and then again on Saturday—Nepal's church day (the only day off).

On Easter Sunday morning we and the whole church squashed into a bus along with the groom, and headed for the wedding four hours away in Surkhet. The pastor had thoughtfully provided us with boiled eggs and doughnuts for the journey. Boiled eggs? Easter? My mother is English, and I was born and brought up in England. However, my father is a Greek Cypriot and our Greek family have all sorts of traditions. Everyone is given a red-dyed boiled egg outside the Greek Church after the Easter service. On that bus I wanted to crack eggs in the Greek Easter fashion and pronounce "Christos Anesti" but no one knew about pagan egg traditions thankfully, and it didn't make sense to explain. So I enjoyed a Greek Easter very quietly with a white egg instead of a red-dyed one.

Hundreds of people gathered in the simple church building at Surkhet. The bans were read out, the exchange of vows was made (very similar in style to the British, albeit in Nepali) and, lo and behold, Janga and Seema were married!

The bus rattled back into Nepalganj late at night, and everyone was shattered from the big day and long trip. As Janga hadn't had time to find a room to rent for Seema and himself, we suggested they stayed in the upstairs apartment of the house that we were staying in. This house had been offered to us by Australian missionaries who were away. We were very surprised when, after getting off the bus, Janga asked us to take Seema to the house as he would be coming late. I showed Seema the apartment and said goodnight. John and I were fast asleep when we were suddenly woken up by the sound of Janga knocking on the door upstairs calling "Seema, Seema." But she didn't answer. She had locked the door and was fast asleep. This went on for over 15 minutes. A dismayed Janga came down asking me what he should do. I suggested he should sleep in the room next to ours, but John had a "better" idea. He took something (I don't know what), went up and started ramming the door down! I felt so bad for the Australian missionaries' door. It couldn't have been louder or more forceful than when Achilles' men rammed the Trojan wall. Lights were going on in the neighbourhood, but fortunately, just before the door was ruined entirely, Seema heard the banging, woke up and opened it. How's that for a wedding night!

Next morning John, myself, Janga, Seema and Mehul were on our way to Lucknow in India again. We thoroughly enjoyed visiting the amazing Nawab's buildings of Lucknow. But best of all was the haunting experience of seeing the British residency that was besieged and destroyed leaving many dead in 1857. Thinking about that impossible situation, I wondered if such brave and heroic people existed today as they did then.

It was good to get back home. Seema and Janga stayed a few days with us, and then returned to Nepalganj.

21

Money, The Curse and a Crash—written on August 25th, 2013

This has been a very long day and it's still only early afternoon. I came to Kandhmal in Odisha two days ago. Not much has gone right since my arrival. But then again, "...in all things God works for the good of those who love Him, who have been called according to his purpose." Rom. 8:28 NIV.

I do believe that I'm in the middle of something which God is doing, and that it will be good though at the moment there is little evidence of it. I'm sitting now in a very sparsely furnished room being watched by a frail old lady. She and I have just undergone an adventure together that we would rather not have experienced.

The Kui primer was inaugurated last November, and following that I had trained 16 teachers to teach adult literacy using it. They had all started far too many classes than they could cope with, as the pastor, who had organised the event, had underscored the fact that I would give some financial support for every class. I sent this support regularly while in Europe, but because I was away no one could contact me. As soon as we got back to India, I got a call from one teacher telling me that the pastor had distributed part of the first month's support, but nothing in all of the following months. I called the other teachers, and found out that, sadly, this was true. This was the second time a pastor has stolen all the teachers' support money!

I got in contact with a Kui teacher from a college in our town. This man, Saral, has proved to be an invaluable help to me because of all the people he knows here in Kandhmal. His uncle Peter, who is a pastor, is highly respected by many people—probably one reason is that he has never taken money from anyone. He would be able to get me the necessary permit for Kandhmal without a bribe. Saral felt we should go and confront the crooked pastor who, in Indian terms, had kept a huge amount of money. Pastor Peter knew that this man had embezzled money in the name of "ministry" before, and an entire school and hostel had to be closed down. I had no wish to go to Odisha at all. But I felt I owed it to the teachers; most, if not all were living way below the poverty line and really had nothing. This pastor's injustice spurred me on to go there—or rather—come here. Pastor Peter and his nephew, Rajiv, met us in Brahmapur in a kind of Indian Land Rover in which we travelled the four hours to Kandhmal.

First we visited some of the teachers as the crooked pastor was out of town. Each one told us that the pastor had ordered them to close down the classes as I was not sending any support. Yet the pastor had emailed me each time I sent money, thanking me and telling me he had distributed it. This was very sad as there had been near to a 1,000 learners. Some stopped, and some continued. I was very discouraged. I met some of the students;

they all said they wanted to continue. I had to walk to each village as the Land Rover couldn't cross a river because a bridge had collapsed. ("Probably because someone had kept the money for the concrete," I thought to myself). It is, however, a really beautiful part of India and the old women are tattooed on their faces, and wear many silver earrings.

This morning we set out early to "catch" the pastor and give him a surprise visit. I had hoped that due to all the evidence I had, including his many emails, he would admit his wrong, and we could resolve the issue somehow. Instead, he showed me seven or eight papers where the teachers had signed their names for their money. It was laughable and primitive as they were all photocopies from the first month when he had given them something. Only the date at the top had been changed. I was angry. He remained adamant and very obstinate. To cut a long story short, we left, leaving him with the opportunity, as a sign of repentance, to put all the remaining money back on my account for me to sort out; but that was not on his agenda.

I felt very upset. We got back in the Land Rover and Saral said he would drive instead of Rajiv, the usual driver. Pastor Peter was sitting up front next to Saral and Rajiv. Pastor Peter's wife, who we had just met and collected on the way, and I were on the seat behind.

We had travelled about 15 minutes and were in the "middle-of-no-where" when a motorbike came careering towards us at full speed. The motorbike was on a wide bend and on our side of the road. Only a split second passed from first seeing it to the crash. In that tiny moment I got down between the seats and pulled the lady down with me. After the crash there was silence.

We got out and saw that the windscreen of our car was badly smashed and the front was caved in. Young Rajiv, who fortunately had not been driving, was in shock, very distraught and crying uncontrollably.

The bike was a crumpled wreck, and three young men were strewn in all directions. Two of them were laid out and one was trying to sit up. The limbs and whole body of one were jerking in a terrible way. I didn't know what to do so I got down, put my hand on his heart and prayed for Jesus to heal him. He became still and I couldn't feel his pulse. He seemed to be dead. We somehow lifted the young men into the Land Rover, and Saral got it started, and drove off with them back to a small hospital in the town where we had come from. I was left trying to comfort Rajiv and Pastor Peter's wife while the ever-calm and docile Pastor Peter was discussing something with the crowd which had gathered. The crowd was really surprised that we hadn't driven off and left the young men. Finally an auto rickshaw came by, and took Pastor Peter's wife and me back to the town that I was staying in where we both are now.

I just got a call from Saral at the hospital where many anguished relatives had been wailing in mourning. He told me how the one who we thought must be dead had suddenly sprung up off the bench where he had been left, and was up and walking about! The mourning family, after a moment of utter shock and disbelief, began slapping his face and scolding him! The other two had been stitched up, and all were told to go to Brahmapur for scans. So Pastor Peter decided to take them under his wing, and go the four-hour trip with them. I am sure that this will be a great testimony to these fellows as there has been bitter persecution in these villages. It was only afterwards that we realised that absolutely nothing had happened to us—not a scratch or a bruise.

Tomorrow I will attempt to gather the teachers together and try to encourage them. If they wish to continue, I will suggest they only run one class each. We will help them open their own bank accounts.

22

On the Road Again— written in March 2014

Once again I was off to Odisha six months after that difficult visit. I left our town on February 25th on the 5am train to Delhi. At 4:25pm I flew to Bhubaneswar. Our pilot was a pilotess and she got us there twenty minutes early! I spent two nights there, and then took a morning train on the 27th down the coast to Brahmapur. This took only two-and-half hours. There was still much evidence of last summer's cyclone. I was met by Raman and we hurried to the bus station in an auto. We only just made it. Then we travelled to Kandhmal district arriving in a small town six hours later. We took another auto which brought us to the best and biggest house in this town (two rooms and a kitchen).

Raman had been worried sick as to where I would stay, and he decided that this large village or small town looked promising. He had scoured the whole place. When he saw this house, he knocked on the door and simply asked if they were willing to put me up! He had done his line-up work, and now, for a small sum, I had a room with a bathroom as well. It is painted with every colour the shop could possibly have had in store. My room alone is pale green, bright pink, turquoise blue, cream, white and royal blue with brown window frames but no panes. There was a lot of fussing going on. Someone disappeared for a while, and then returned with a bucket, mug, and a new electric rod so that I could have a hot bath. The owner's brother-in-law appeared and wanted to know everything, and altogether five men were fussing around in the room trying to find a socket which would work for the mosquito repellent device. None did, so they found me a pink mosquito net, reminding me that this was a malaria region (not that anyone else used the nets that were lying around). Dinner arrived in various aluminium canisters.

On my last visit, I was at the lowest point of all my endeavours when all the trained teachers had stopped their classes due to that crooked pastor, who had kept eight months of their support money for himself.

Raman, the only one of the old group, had decided to train 12 people himself. But I had inwardly given up, with no more hope for Kandhmal even after all the effort I had put into writing a primer in the Kui language.

He had phoned me about a month ago, pleading with me to come and see this new batch of teachers teaching. Somehow I knew I had to go or else it would be my own fault if they really were moving ahead, and then stopped due to my disinterest. If you don't know these people, you can't appreciate how downtrodden and supressed they are, which is why they tend to give up. The work is difficult for the best of people, and they are on the limits of survival.

All the teachers were coming to meet me for the first time next day. The plan was to ask about the classes, get their feedback, give a refresher course, and then over the next six days visit every class. My next plan was to completely finish all the corrections on Book Two of the primer with the original typist.

So next day I was expecting to start with a short devotion, but when I got to the village they had been singing for an hour already, and I found myself in a church service instead of a literacy meeting. Not only the 12 teachers but the whole congregation were present, and **I** was giving the message. This was not exactly our family policy. I shared about the woman at the well, and why Jesus chose to reveal His Messiahship to her rather than to the religious people around Him. Afterwards, I got a really good response. Two in the meeting were Hindus who then talked with key people of the church about following Jesus! The church had provided some of the food and I also provided some, so we could all eat together afterwards. It was good to see about 40 people well fed for at least one day.

The literacy meeting went well. It was followed by Raman bringing his class together, and him teaching the up-to-date lesson 17 in Kui Book One. The 15 students read the story eagerly. I was so happy. Afterwards, I was given a tour of this village. If I say that the people have nothing, I mean that they have a house of mud or brick with a tin roof. A house is altogether about eight square feet. They have two or three cooking vessels and a mat to sleep on, and that's it. The village is very clean probably because they have no rubbish to throw away. About ten families are active Christians and 30 families are animist. If a man works for the government e.g. in road building, he earns Rs100 to Rs150 a day. If it is for a private person, he earns only Rs70 a day (about one

Swiss franc or one USA dollar). They eat rice and lentils. They are gentle, peaceful and kind people.

The next six days.

The next six days were a perpetual shock! Of the 12 teachers only two were unable to teach. I was so thrilled to see their capabilities! The smallest group had 15 students. In one place two classes had been joined together for the day as two brothers were the teachers at the same village. This village was one hour distance in the auto from the last village, and everyone came to the class. Only the teachers are Christians and the villagers are Hindus. The brothers have very strong hopes that, as they read the Bible stories and talk together as a group, the whole lot may turn to Christ.

On another day we were in the auto rickshaw and passed by this village again, and then we drove another 20 minutes or so. After this we had to walk down a mountain. It was pouring with rain. This teacher was the most ardent of all. But this Christian hamlet was also the poorest by far. Electricity had never come to this handful of houses. On that day it was just as well as lightning was striking all around us. The village was too far from a school so this class was made up of everyone: babies, children and parents, young and old alike. We all somehow fitted into a four-by-seven foot room, and had to wait for the rain to stop so we could dry the floor to sit on it (because of the leaking roof). All the people were so excited to be reading and, of course, I was thrilled. The teacher told me that every house there had been burned to the ground during the persecution.

Including Raman's, I visited 12 teachers and their classes. The 150 to 200 or so students told me that they had never learned to read before. This was a whole new dimension in their lives. I freely told people how I became a Christian when I was 13 years old after the Gideons had given me a New Testament. They were very excited, and anticipated being able to read about Jesus for themselves.

I spent the last two or three days finishing the Kui Book Two with Raman, who originally did all the illustrations, and Bubu the typist. It was laborious work, but also exciting to get all the corrections finished and done with. We completed everything just one hour before my night bus back to Bhubaneswar.

I had miraculously received ten days permission to enter the area from the chief collector. It is nearly impossible to get even three days for a foreigner to go to Kandhmal. I have certainly never seen a foreigner in these parts. So I really praise God for this privilege and for having such a blessed time.

23

Visit of the Transvestites— written in early 2014

Every time we made each one of our rented houses liveable with windows and doors actually opening and closing, and bathrooms and toilets draining and flushing as they were meant to, the landlord claimed his house back, wanting it for his own use. So we decided to build a house of our own. Obviously this was no small thing in India, and John definitely turned a stark shade of grey during the building process. However, it was all finally finished, and we had just begun revelling in the feeling of being threat-free when our peace was challenged.

At the beginning, in our new house, we had a helper for a short while—a Christian lady from our tiny village who came and washed dishes three times a week. We were doing something in the kitchen one morning when the doorbell rang. Without a thought I went to open it and there, like a picture framed in the doorway, stood three transvestites, fat and pouring out of their clothes. They pressed right through into the living room. The three of them with their masculine, muscular bodies with women's breasts and part male, part female faces, heavily made up, were gesticulating like travelling comedians. They were banging massive drums and wanted money.

We had built a house and now, common to their custom, they had come to demand their "rights". Being totally unaware of their habits and customs, I couldn't understand why Esther, our helper, was looking so distraught and praying in a loud voice to Jesus. I tried to make them get out, but they slid into a role which they must have played hundreds of times. They started with tart smiles, and shifted into an emotional frenzy demanding money and lots of it! John looked equally bewildered when he came downstairs.

"Well—give them ten rupees to get rid of them," he said. Ten rupees! They literally fell on the floor laughing.

"Ten thousand rupees at least!" they cried.

Esther told us, "Yes you have to give it them because you have built a house. They will curse you otherwise."

John got really mad, and this was mirrored on their faces. One took up my guitar, and holding it by the neck, began swinging it towards John. I pleaded with "her" not to destroy it as it was very precious to me and "she" seemed to melt into another character, weeping for the guitar. I carefully unwound "her" handbag chain that had become entangled around the neck of the guitar, and gently removed "her" hands from the instrument. Another one began a hysterical performance insulting John by removing all "her" lower clothes and displaying "herself" before him. Esther, hands up in the air in disbelief, turned away disgusted, praying louder than ever, while the others thoroughly enjoyed the effect. I hardly knew what to do. Reasoning didn't help, and trying to push them out also didn't help as they were much bigger and stronger than us. Finally I decided to walk out and, sure enough, they followed me. When they could see that we had no fear of them, they began raining curses down on us.

They said, "All Indians give us money, but you foreigners never do."

We told them that as Christians we had nothing to fear, so they could jump and gyrate and curse as much as they liked—it wouldn't get them anywhere. They got into their brand new car and, in a furious rage, drove off. But we knew we had gained a spiritual victory.

Transvestites dance in trains and confined spaces, and then beg off the passengers. Just about no one denies them money as they are greatly revered. These pathetic creatures make a lot of money playing on peoples' fears. They turn up when a mother has just given birth, and threaten to take the baby and "doctor it" to make it like one of them, if money is not handed over. It is not uncommon for babies to disappear in this way. They turn up at weddings and, in our case, at homes which have just been built. The worst of it is that the government assures them of their so called "rights" so they have the full cover of Indian law.

Fear and superstition rules the hearts of people in this country. Hindus are fertile ground to breed the superstition that the religion thrives on to exist.

24

The Lord's Protection— written in May 2015

I thank the Lord for His continued protection over these last few years in India.

Once we had travelled down to Delhi to meet our daughter. The three of us were taking a train to go and visit Rajasthan together. At first we were heading for New Delhi railway station when the auto rickshaw driver told us that the Rajasthan trains normally go from Old Delhi. We checked our tickets and he was right, so we changed our route. At the very moment we arrived in Old Delhi station, a massive bomb went off at New Delhi station killing many people.

While in Rajasthan we visited a very famous fort which used to be the palace of the Maharajas of Jodhpur. Within the palace fort is a temple which we refrained from visiting but we were standing right by its walls. Just a couple of days later over 1,000 devotees had gathered at that same spot waiting to catch a glimpse of the deity. When the temple doors were opened there was a stampede and 147 people were killed and many injured.

Another time John and I had to go to West Bengal. He was going for Bible teaching and I was going for Teacher Training Workshops.

We had ordered an auto rickshaw to come and take the three of us (John, our daughter and me) to the station at 5am. When it arrived our neighbour, who was also leaving for a trip in his car, insisted that we ride with him to the station. So the auto went on its way. A thick fog had descended in the night, and our neighbour didn't see the concrete divider in the middle of the road, and ploughed right into it. The car had a great hole in it, and oil and water were gushing out from under the engine. Fortunately, we were unharmed. We walked the rest of the way with our luggage to the station. When we arrived eight hours later in Delhi there was much alarm at the station; people and TV cameras were rushing around as the breaking news came in that there had been five train accidents (all collisions) due to the fog. Two were on our route and a number of people had been killed. However, we left from Delhi on time, but had to change route on the way. It took over 40 hours to get there.

In West Bengal, John had several meetings with local pastors, but the meetings came to a halt because there was an elephant roaming about. It had broken down a brick wall of someone's kitchen to get to the salt. As nobody wanted to take any risks, the meetings abruptly ended.

Just a couple of weeks earlier, a young man who had been a member of the church choir, was trampled to death by an elephant in the same area. Villagers had been flashing lights at a group of elephants to scare them away from the rice fields. One elephant panicked and the young man had been in the way. A few days after the tragedy, the elephant returned with more elephants. They held each other's tails and circled the spot where the man had died.

While still in the vicinity, John and a pastor had to lead a Bible Study. They each were driving a motor bike, and each having a passenger behind them. It was dark after the Bible Study and, of course, there were no street lamps in those areas. John's bike lights were quite poor, which made driving something of a challenge, especially as the road was full of pot holes. As he was intensely concentrating on the pot holes, John wondered why the pastor on the motor bike in front suddenly made a huge curve in a spot where the road seemed to be fine. He had swerved right over the two-lane highway and then carried on. Thinking he was perfectly safe, and not seeing any pot holes there, John continued straight on. Then the passenger behind suddenly started shouting,

"Elephant, elephant!" And right there, where John had not made a curve, was an elephant about to cross the road. He had driven right under its neck! He had seen something in the corner of his eye, but had mistaken it for one of the many large bushes.

Another incident with animals was here at home. One morning John was outside in the garden. He had just gone round the corner of the house where the back garden opens up, and there sprawled on the garden wall was the most amazing and beautiful leopard! They saw each other at the same moment with less than two metres between them. The leopard got up and leapt down on the side of the forested hill, and was gone in an instant.

25

Priya—written in June 2015

In December 2014 I found myself in Nepal: a forced exit from India pursuing the illusive visa. This problem has plagued us since we no longer could get longer-term student visas. I made the most of my time by holding a Teacher Training Workshop for eight Nepalese teacher trainees in Nepalganj.

One of the participants was Priya—a tall, lean young woman. She managed the method of the training very well. She told me that she was suffering a lot of physical pain due to her abusive husband. As I got to know her she revealed that they made their living by building retaining walls. These are the really heavy-duty stone walls which dam or divert the flow of rivers. Both she and her husband worked on the construction of these walls and, when she heard that I lived in a town of North India known to her, she told me that they often came to work there.

Two months later I got a call from her. She said that they were working on a wall in our town. She phoned several times, and so one evening John and I went to see her. It was the end of January and very cold at night. Their employer had given them a roughly built room, without windows, which was partly below ground where the mud floor was wet and slimy. In there, her parents-in-law, some other family members, Priya, her husband and children had erected their black plastic tents in the corners of the room. We climbed into the room which was in pitch darkness except for a small fire where her husband was squatting. Her two children, a girl of about eight and a boy of about six, were also there. The living conditions were terrible. The next day I found a quilt and other warm items and took them to her.

A few days later the job on that site had come to an end, and they had their plastic tents pitched directly on a river bed where they were building another wall. Priya told me how her husband had got drunk again the night before, and together with his *golis* (tablets) and other drugs— *bang* which is a stronger type of marijuana plant— he had gone off his head and beaten her badly. He had then disappeared for the night, reappeared in the morning, taken all the money that they had, and left. He returned later in the day having bought for himself an expensive jacket while the family had no money for food.

I offered her work in our house once a week to get respite from the heavy labour and abuse, and to earn some more money. She was a very efficient and faithful worker. I contacted a Christian group similar to Alcoholics Anonymous. They agreed to come with us, and meet her husband to encourage him to get help. He remained silent as they talked. They ended up by telling him that it was up to him, and if he decided in favour of getting help he just needed to make the phone call. He never did. Priya came to church a couple of times as she is a strong believer. She managed to bring her husband once as well. When they were newlyweds ten years earlier, they had both made a commitment to follow Christ, but he was very weak minded.

Week after week, in every spare moment while Priya was in our house, she would beg us to help her and the children to find refuge away from this man. Each Friday she unloaded her frustration and anguish about the latest event; each time, a new drama had unfolded. The stories of his abuse and alcoholism were unlimited. He had broken her arm at one stage, and when she went to hospital they didn't want to treat her. Finally they put the arm in plaster but before she got home the plaster had fallen off! Her husband's younger sister of 17 years, who also lived with them, had been told by her parents to encourage men to visit her. And so, from one day to the next, his sister switched from wall-builder to prostitute. This was better money.

Because I had got to know Priya in a teacher training set-up, I had always related to her on a different level to that of a domestic worker. She was bright, capable and reliable and had become a friend.

One night at 1:30am she called me, pleading for us to come and rescue her. We had been asleep, and also knew that we had to pick up our daughter and her husband from the station at 5am. Still we couldn't ignore her. We went but she didn't appear. We waited but nothing happened. Later that day, at 9am, she came and told us her husband had gone "mad" again while everyone was sleeping. He had set fire to the tent with her and the children inside. The family was trying to stop him; he was swinging a rod and beating everyone including Priya and his parents. The children had run for their lives, and when they eventually came back they were in a state of shock. So when we got there she didn't want to rock the boat anymore, and didn't come out of the tent. Also the day before, her young son had watched his auntie (the prostitute) have an abortion in their tent which had also freaked him out.

She begged us to find her a hostel or a school for the children where she would also be able to work and be in a safe, protected environment.

We did ask pastors and other local Christian workers, and although there are so many of these institutions for such desperate people, we did not receive any response or help from anyone.

My daughter and son-in-law reminded us of an institution in Andhra Pradesh where they had worked for a year. This is a beautiful hospital and school which is supported from abroad and is very well equipped, where teams of young people from USA come to engage with the students every year. Not only does the school focus on the uplifting of underprivileged children, but has gained a reputation in the state for its high standard of education, winning prizes from the government. Priya got very excited about it when we told her. The children would at last go to school and even study in English medium. This is something a family in their position could only dream of. So I contacted the president of the organisation. He is an American of India descent, who is also the president of a renowned business school in California. He has become a friend of ours through our daughter.

He welcomed Priya and her children with open arms. She would be able to work there either in the school or at the hospital. They would get their education, food and accommodation free and she would receive a small wage. It was a dream-come-true! He warned that her husband must not know of her whereabouts and that she must come with a long-term commitment to enable her children to graduate. We showed her videos of the school and put the conditions to her in no uncertain terms. We encouraged her to think about it. She herself said she wanted to pray about it and that if she had no peace she would know it was not of the Lord. I didn't expect to hear from her for a week but, before four days had passed, she called saying she was sure and ready to go. Now we were all faced with the problem of how she would do the actual leaving.

As John was booked to go to West Bengal the following week we organised the tickets for her and the children to travel on the same train as far as Delhi. We bought her tickets for the train journey all the way to the last stop before the town in Andhra Pradesh.

The greatest worry was how to leave without her husband or the family noticing. He would obviously stop her, and another violent scene would ensue. As the train was at 5am we told her that she needed to leave the day before. I knew that if we brought them to our house this would be the first place he would come to, and the plan would be lost. I asked some friends but, probably out of fear, they would not take them. I suggested to her that they go to one of the hotels by the railway station, but she adamantly refused. Of course, such an idea would be so foreign to her, and the hotel staff might abuse her. I was getting very desperate on the morning of "the day before". Literally, at the last minute, a young couple from our church spontaneously agreed to take them.

Priya told us how she ended up packing all their things in front of her wide-eyed parents-in-law. She told them she couldn't bear this life anymore and that she was going to her brother in

Gujarat state. I don't know where her husband was at this point. She and the children took an auto which brought them near to our house. As John was on his way to the hospital for a small operation at the very same time, I met them, and put them in the car and sped to our friend's house. We arranged that we would come for them at 4am the next day to go to the station. I remember feeling very nervous.

John returned home from the hospital and, about half an hour, later her husband arrived at our house on the back of a motorbike with a friend. I couldn't bring myself to lie about anything. He looked livid when I answered the door, and he told me of Priya's disappearance. I went inside and called John. He asked for Priya's phone number which John gave him. It was the number she had had these past few weeks. Her husband had smashed his own phone two weeks earlier and had chewed up the SIM card! We had given her my old phone and SIM at that time. He said he was going to Gujarat, and then he left.

Something struck me as very strange when we went to get Priya and children at 4am. They were fast asleep! I was still nervous as I knew her husband was not very far away. We waited half an hour outside, and finally the dishevelled trio appeared in the darkness. Later our friends told me how she had been on the phone a lot with her brother and husband—something we had warned her against. I asked our friends to accompany us as I would be returning alone, and I was afraid the husband was near the station. However, neither came with me. I dropped John, Priya and her children off before the station entrance, and waited for John's call to say they were all on the train. To my relief, her husband had not guessed she would be on that train.

John phoned from Delhi to tell me how he had got them to the other station in Delhi, and had settled them in a shady place where they would have to wait from 11am until 11pm for their next train. Just as he was leaving them to catch his own train to West Bengal, a pastor appeared out of nowhere and offered to help them as he was also going to the same railway station as they were! We were so thankful and knew the Lord was sending people to help her.

From Delhi it was a two-day and two-night trip. The lovely administrator of the school and hospital was in constant touch with Priya to ease her anxiety. He speaks Hindi well as he is from a North-East state. He organised a personal friend to meet her at the railway station where the pastor had to leave them, and so she and her children were well cared for throughout their journey.

I was so thrilled and relieved when he called to say they had finally arrived. When I talked briefly with her I was taken aback when she complained about the long journey and didn't have anything positive to say. We put it down to the great upheaval. I was puzzled nevertheless.

In the meantime I had nervously been anticipating a visit from her husband, and sure enough, a few days later I got one. It was quite scary because a whole group of people arrived on motorbikes, and it was dark at 8pm. Thinking it was a neighbour who was ringing the bell, I was dismayed to see all these men, although I also noticed the mother-in-law amongst them. They were demanding a "talk". I told them that I was alone and that they should not have come at that time. I said they should return when my husband got back at the end of the month. But they wouldn't go. I stayed inside, but phoned my neighbours who were the only believers in our village and lived right opposite. I let them deal with it. A crowd had gathered, and the group (which the husband's family had rallied together) started demanding Priya's phone number. From the veranda I told them I had already given it to her husband (who was not amongst them). Not satisfied, they then began demanding money! Surprise, surprise! Every dispute here revolves around money. I knew they had no interest in Priya or the children. They had been trying to push her into prostitution recently. By now half of our village had gathered and, though I knew they would deal with this as they would not tolerate a group of mostly men disturbing a woman alone at night, I was pretty scared. Those supporting Priya's husband didn't give up easily. They left after about one and half hours.

Next morning at 7am the bell rang again. Fortunately, this time it was only her parents-in-law and one other woman. Apparently Priya's husband was already in Gujarat at her brother's place, furious at not finding her there. Again they were demanding a phone number and again I gave them the same response. My Christian neighbours, the village chief and the friends who had put Priya up for the night, gathered round. While we were discussing their son's rages, wild behaviour and abuse, the father-in-law suddenly produced a slip of paper with a phone number on it. Totally perplexed I asked whose it was.

"Priya's," they replied. As she was in a different state she had a new SIM card. She had called them four days earlier and given them her new number. Defying logic, they still sat staring indifferently at me.

"So let's phone her up then," I said. We called and they were able to talk with her. The tension dissolved, and they got up and left. We laughed at their ploy to try to pressurise me. I learned a valuable lesson—never to give in to these stalemate situations. Force them to give way. Then the truth comes out. They knew where she was and contacting her hadn't been an issue. They haven't been back since. Slowly my friends and I realised that Priya was not keeping to the agreement: that her husband should not know of her whereabouts.

Meanwhile the administrator was very disappointed at Priya's behaviour. She was actually complaining about the food! I knew that it was infinitely better than anything they had ever known. According to her, the children wanted to go "home". She said that, actually her husband was a good man, and could he join them?

A couple of days went by and the administrator gave her a big chance. Seeing as she had told her husband where she was, he said, "Let your husband come on May 26th as the president of the institution is also coming on that day from USA, and perhaps something can be negotiated." But then Priya decided she hated the place and just wanted to return. So after a few more days that's what she did.

Though they are probably back in our town in their plastic tent in 40° Celsius heat, we have decided not to have contact with them. Sometimes enough is enough.

26

Finally—written in December 2015

At the time of writing there are now 36 classes running in the district of Kandhmal, Odisha. Each class has a minimum of ten students, usually about 15, some with Christian students, some Hindu, and often they are a mix of the two. There are more on-going classes in other parts of Odisha and in other Indian states— some of which I have mentioned, some I haven't—and not least in our town. I have given teacher training along with a colleague to other Christian groups. I have no knowledge of whether those people went on to teach or not. Work among the Muslim Gujjar has been difficult, partly because they are a semi-nomadic people.

The success of this work is due to the personal passion of the literacy teachers who are carefully selected. Each teacher is given a monthly honorarium. When each volume is successfully taught and learned–each within six months (I'm a hard checker!)— I give them a happy bonus.

At a time when "progressive India" is known in the western world for its high-tech and information technology expertise, it speaks volumes that literacy has not yet come to vast numbers of people in India. This is not only because of the gross neglect of large and small tribal groups and contempt for women and girls, but also due to superstition, religious and cultural barriers as well as gross corruption.

Indians generally don't read. Of course, there are the exceptions and I know one or two of them. Is it a lack of good books in their own language? Maybe. Those who feel at home in English tend to be the more enthusiastic readers but, by and large, Indians prefer to be entertained with television or other social media. Happily there is a difference among many if not most Christians: they want to read God's Word i.e. the Bible. This wonderful phenomenon in India sets them apart from the rest. In rural India it is often the case that the only time you see literacy being applied is in the church during Bible study, women's meetings and worship services.

The illiterate Christians are usually highly motivated, and having experienced salvation are eager to get to know their Lord. It creates a new kind of people regardless of their tribe or caste. It makes others incredibly jealous of them too. As I bring this book to a close I am once again in Kandhmal having checked many classes using reading and writing tests. In a few days' time we will have a celebration of music, tribal dancing, good food and prize giving. Ninety people have successfully completed both volumes of the primer this year, and for each their prize will be a Bible. It will be the first book they have ever possessed and they are very excited.

The government reserves seats in higher education for tribal and scheduled castes, and also allocates desirable posts in the work place to them.

Sounds wonderful. But not so for the Christians of Kandhmal. If you're a Christian, you are bypassed and on the local level you may only get jobs as hired hands for landowners or as labourers building or fixing roads.

When William Carey came to India in 1793 he was shunned by the British East India Company, and so was forced to seek refuge in Serampore –then a Danish enclave in Bengal close to Kolkata. His life's work was that of translating the Holy Scriptures into numerous Indian as well as foreign languages[1]. The British East India Company knew that knowledge of the Bible brought knowledge of right and wrong. It opened the way to a moral change of heart, the transition from fear and superstition to peace, assurance and trust in a living, loving God. All of this was detrimental to the aggressive trade they were doing with the submissive, ignorant Indians of that time. I was shocked to learn that vast numbers of Indians, even in Bengal, are still illiterate today. What is the use of these translated Bibles if the people cannot read? That is why I believe literacy is the way forward.

Humanists and many who think that man is good at heart try to convince us that we can better ourselves by ourselves. Only a few years ago westerners were actually saying that we were heading towards a better world. Education is thought by many to be the answer to becoming a happier and a better person. But it isn't. History proves it. It is a means to an end, not an end in itself.

---

[1] William Carey's Biblical translations are as follows: the whole Bible— Bengali, Oriya, Hindi, Marathi, Sanskrit and Assamese; Punjabi New Testament and Old Testament up to Ezekiel 26; Pashto and Kashmiri New Testament and Old Testament up to 2 Kings; Telegu and Konkani New Testament and Pentateuch; the New Testament in 19 other languages; and one or more Gospels in five more languages.

Christ is the only One who can change the hearts and minds of us fickle human beings. That is why He said that His Kingdom is not of this world, and to His followers He said that the Kingdom of God is within us. It is my experience that God's living Word the "Christ" or "Messiah" has proved Himself to be true over and over again. Whole families—even whole villages—have been changed by His compelling love. Who would want anything else? You have to live here to see the difference.

Come Back Lord Jesus

Come back, come back Lord Jesus
And complete your work on earth.
Come back, come back Lord Jesus
And complete your life in us.
Come back, come back Lord Jesus
And complete your promise to the world.

The time is coming, waiting has been long
But the moment we've longed for arrives,
When the Lord will silence the defiance of the gods
With His presence and His piercing eyes.

The nations will see the awesome sight
Not shock but shame will overwhelm,
And His children will rise on the wings of the wind,
Called out of earth to a higher realm.

Come back, come back Lord Jesus
And complete your work on earth
Come back, come back Lord Jesus
And complete your life in us.
Come back, come back Lord Jesus
And complete your promise to the world.

a song, written by the author.

Glossary

Adivasi—a term for a heterogeneous set of ethnic and tribal groups considered to be the aboriginal population.

Betel nut—Areca nut-seed of betel palm which when chewed with leaves of the betel pepper and lime causes it to turn red. Used as a digestive stimulant and narcotic.

Bhajan—Hindu chant.

Brahmin—highest caste in Hinduism; specializing as priests, religious teachers and protectors of sacred learning.

Caste—in Hinduism a hereditary social class among Hindus; stratified according to ritual purity.

Diwali— the main Hindu festival of the year where prayers are typically offered to Lakshmi, the goddess of wealth and prosperity; also known as the Festival of Light.

Imam—the man who leads prayers in a mosque; for Shiites an Imam is a recognised authority on Islamic theology and law and a spiritual guide.

Kama Sutra—Hindu sex manual.

Koran—the Islamic sacred book.

Mullah—a Muslim trained in the doctrine and law of Islam; the head of a mosque.

Naxalite—a member of a Communist guerrilla group; the term Naxal derives from the name of the village Naxalbari in West Bengal where the movement had its origin.

N.G.O.—non-government organisation.

Paan—a concoction of betel nut, lime and spices wrapped in the betel pepper leaf, chewed as a stimulant turning all the juices red which are then spat everywhere.

Peon—messenger, runner, menial worker in an office.

Prasaad—food offered to idols.

Puja—ritualistic Hindu worship.

Salwar Kurta—Indian and Pakistani loose fitting cotton pyjama-like pants with long collarless shirt worn over them.

Scheduled Caste—official designation given to various groups of historically disadvantaged indigenous people.

Thugee — Hindi word for deceit. Refers to the acts of **Thugs**, an organised gang of professional robbers and murderers. Entered the English language and is used to mean an aggressive and violent young criminal.

Recommended Reading

<u>From Kandhamal to Karavali: The Ugly Face of Sangh Parivar</u> . This is a fact- finding report of nine Human Rights Organisations that visited Orissa and Karnataka from September to October, 2008. The underlined is an internet link.

"William Carey" by S Pearce Carey.

Printed in the United States
By Bookmasters